11-17-23

Ageless!

Never Too Old,
Never Too Late

Judith Horky

Ageless!

Never Too Old, Never Too Late

By Judith Horky

Copyright © 2014

First Printing January 2014

ISBN: 978-0-9711862-3-1

Published by
Crystal Mountain Press
Pagosa Springs, CO 81147

http://www.JudithHorky.com

Printed in the United States of America

ACKNOWLEDGMENTS

My heartfelt thanks to Sam Hunneman and Annie Miller for their invaluable help and for their wonderful Ageless skills and attitudes.

My deep gratitude and love to my wonderful, understanding husband, Jim!

Dedicated to
Victoria Smith, my young-at-heart cousin,
and
To all women of all ages who are
Never too old!

Contents

INTRODUCTION

Growing old is not the end of the world, or the end of the fun, or fulfillment, or even sex. Sure, the older we get, the more things can go wrong with our bodies and our lives. We have crises to face, big and small, but the way we deal with them is the key.

So we mourn the dreams and goals of years past — cast aside, unfulfilled — because now we're afraid it's too late to do anything about them. To top that off, the older we get, the faster time flies. So many things take precedence in our lives ... school, jobs, mates, pregnancy, babies, moving, broken water pipes, broken bones, kids who have pushed us to the wall/limit ... even politics! You name it.

Maybe you've looked in the mirror and wondered who is that wrinkled woman staring back at you. She reminds you of your mother, or worse, your grandmother. You lean closer to scrutinize the ravages of time. Not a good idea! Deep down, you know your reflection is not a true image of the real, *much younger* woman who dwells inside that lovely patina façade, but damn! Everything is heading south! Stretch marks, subtle drooping of the intimate parts of your body, nasty cellulite ... the panoramic view is just too much.

In our alone moments, we've lamented, "No! I don't want to grow old!" Confess it. Go ahead. Say it right out loud. How could Mother Nature be so cruel? Life's been tough and you've earned the right to be depressed once in a while, right? Of course you have. But the fact is, we—you and I—need to fix whatever is fixable and enjoy the satisfaction of knowing we can. And yes, it helps—in fact, it's darn near imperative—to have the support and love of close friends, sometimes family if you're lucky, who will listen to, *and honor*, your feelings during the process.

The good news is that many women today, young and old alike, are experiencing a surge of strength and power. They're working at owning their own space and making choices based on the power of that ownership. But not all of us. Breaking free can oftentimes lead to frustration and unhappiness.

It's possible to overcome life's struggles, but to do so requires opening the doors marked Emotional, Spiritual, Physical and Mental. It's time to move into a loving life filled with plenty of laughter. On the following pages, you'll read about real life experiences—some mine, and some other women's — which will give you the insight to change from "Damn, I'm getting old!" to "I've only just begun!" *It's never too late and you're never too old!* Now, go get a cuppa tea, a latté or a glass of wine and let's go!

~ONE~

*"Whether you think you can or think you can't,
you are right."*

Henry Ford

Are You Willing to Change?

Indeed, do you *want* to change? Are you *willing* to change? Hmmm. Those may sound like easy questions, but changing requires us to look at our own resistance and examine those automatic responses to any suggestions to do things unfamiliar to us. I'm hearing, "Yes, but ..." and "Of course I am ... but." So take a deep breath and get off your "but" before it sabotages the whole process.

My desire for independence was—*is*—strong. Not that many years ago, I experienced a deep-seated need to depend only on myself ... I should say "my *self*". Two words, the second interchangeable with "my soul." I spent years struggling to find some form of independence, to be able to acknowledge myself as a worthy

11

individual, capable of something besides being a good wife and mother. Understand, please, that I'm not denigrating either of those roles. Both have given me enormous satisfaction and pride. However, while fulfilling them, I, like so many other women, slowly lost or gave away whatever sense of self I had. I didn't realize how lost I was until I finally reached outside the image I had allowed myself to be shoehorned into. The process — my spiritual interment, if you will — was insidious, and for years, I really had no idea it was happening.

Granted, for many women, independence creates great fear. We were raised with a deep, basic expectation that *someone* would take care of us. That scenario goes like this: "I want my freedom to experience life, to earn income and experience job satisfaction ... and by the way, when will your paycheck be here to pay the mortgage and buy the groceries? And by the way, I don't like being alone too long, so don't go away ... and when you come home, the door knob needs fixing, the weeds are overgrown, and I can't lift the heavy things out of the back of the car." Not exactly independent living happening here!

A majority of women — although certainly not all — went from having a male caregiver to protect them, straight to marriage, or a live-in relationship with a full bag of expectations. Even if we spent time on our own in the world, working at a real job and making our own decisions, we still knew deep down that if things got rough, we weren't going to be allowed to sink. Dad would throw out the old life preserver and we could hang on until we stabilized again. Marriage replaced Dad in that respect. And that was the slippery slope upon which our much-desired independence soon lost its footing, on that happy slide into family, community, societal and marital obligations.

So time marches on. Some women choose to work or they have to; some make other choices. And every once in a while, we experience an overwhelming desire to just stretch; to achieve our own independence, to care for ourselves, without the constant background noise which is our desire to take care of everyone else, too. We push and pull with our emotions and our mate, often severing relationship ties because, being so strongly wrapped in expectations and demands, any capacity for compromise has been lost long ago.

In relationships, growing out of *I-need-to-be-with-you-and-I-can't-survive-without-you* into *I-want-to-be-with-you-but-I-**can**-survive-without-you* is a major leap over dark chasms of uncertainty and off rocky cliffs into the unknown. One's life may or may not be turned upside down in the process, but once again, the reward of finding 'self' makes it worth the risk. That reward is called independence.

So we finally reach the "real" world, full of hopes, the exhilaration of freedom, excitement, and ... Wham! All those "little" details ... the rent, the home repairs, car noises and family emergencies, become huge, scary dinosaurs, and our newfound independence finds itself standing right in their path.

And that's the time to get painfully honest. Make a list. (I know. I hate lists, too, but it's the best way to start.) Just how *would* you like your life to be different? What, exactly, do *you* want? No one will see your answers, so be specific and remember to check behind *all* the doors— Emotional, Spiritual, Physical and Mental. There's no need to limit yourself.

Depending on your age and stage in life, there may be as many answers as old Mr. Carter had Little Liver Pills, and they're all important to you. Expect to be influenced in your choices by the time of day, how you slept last night, if you've eaten too much spicy food, or had one more drink than you should have had. Even the behavior of your mate or kids or co-workers can skew the results. In other words, the simple acts of everyday living can definitely affect how you feel about certain aspects of your life and, therefore, what you come up with off the top of your head.

Continue adding to or subtracting from your lists, and you'll eventually discover there are some things that reappear, again and again. Number them, starting with Most Important. This will shift too, depending on your mood (which fluctuates a lot during menopause … just a warning), but this paring down and homing in on what you truly want in your life is critically necessary.

So let's go deeper. Embrace the concept that you do create your own reality. Like it or not, your life is what you make of it, influenced by your thoughts and feelings. As the age-old saying goes, "Be careful what you wish for because you're likely to get it." It's absolutely amazing how our thoughts, whether negative or positive, put the wheels in motion to create what we're thinking about. Thoughts do become things.

Make time for honest reflection: Let's start with some mental time traveling. Find a quiet, peaceful place. Relax. Maybe even light a candle, and allow yourself to go back, back, back …

"I will not, I cannot, I don't want to ever date again!"

I was 44 when my divorce was final. Several years before, I'd returned to college as an older student, since my *working for money* was unacceptable to my first husband. He was the breadwinner. I was a stay-at-home mom, a position that was considered a high honor in the 50s and 60s. (I wouldn't trade my time with my children, but the negative results sure do hit hard when it comes to collecting social security!)

So, since going back to college was acceptable, and since I'd wallpapered and painted everything but the kids—multiple times—I was more than ready for change. But realizing that I would be one of the oldest students on campus added to the nightmare of having to memorize facts and figures, and being seriously confidence-deprived, enrolling and showing up took a good deal of courage. And that was before I got to the social scene …

You see, I was sure I'd be living my new life as a celibate, middle-aged matron, because through the years, my self-esteem had been pretty well demolished and my self-image was … well, "celibate, middle-aged matron" sort of says it all. My younger classmates, though? They had different ideas!

"Never date again? That's the most ridiculous thing I've ever heard!" said Tracy sipping her Coke. The campus commissary was filled with young beautiful bodies that emphasized my fears.

"Come on, Judy. Get a life. You're attractive, fun, got a good figure. You won't have any problems. You've got to change your attitude and go for it!"

"I can't change who I am, Tracy. I have three sons, one in college and two still in high school. I was a virgin when I got married. I'm a little tender on the rejection thing." I shook my head. *"Nope. Don't even think about it."*

She leaned across the table, definitely in my face. "I am picking you up tomorrow night at 8 p.m. A bunch of us are going dancing and you're coming with us. You can sit and watch if you want, but be ready by eight and wear your jeans and cowboy boots. Got it?"

"Yes, but ..."

"No buts. Be ready." And she was gone.

I was old enough to be her mother for heaven's sake! But I bit the bullet. Scared? Yes. Embarrassed? You bet. Wishing I was staying at home in bed with a good book? Absolutely. She zipped up at 8 o'clock in her old but incredibly speedy Porsche. I wondered what my more conventional neighbors thought as we hit 60 mph in our cul-de-sac. I was plastered to the back of my seat, but laughing.

And you know, I had a really good time. The music was great and I was asked to dance by guys of all ages, shapes, and sizes. I fell in love with the country swing music of "Asleep at the Wheel" and decided I was willing to make a change after all. (I still love that band and dancing!)

This was a huge step outside the box for me, one that gave me the courage to at least leave the house. No doubt about it, friends are invaluable. About a month later, I met the girls for another Coke and some much-needed advice.

"Okay," I began, actually blushing. I was told later that I'd had the look of a deer caught in the headlights. I took a deep breath and continued, "I'm dating. But this is 1979 and things are so different from the fifties. I'm going out to dinner with this guy for the third time and … um, well, um, do I have to sleep with him now?"

Incredulous looks and hysterical laughter had me thinking that I should just crawl under the table. But they quieted down (with only an occasional giggle) when they realized I was dead serious.

"Hey, relax girl. You can do whatever you want. It's different now. You are a woman and you can make choices. Is he cute? Do you like him?"

I lowered my lashes demurely. "Well, as a matter of fact, yes, he's cute and he's a great skier. But he's at least ten years younger than I am. I have wrinkles. I'm scared to death. I don't want …"

"Stop right there. For crying out loud, you need to change your thinking, Judy. Enjoy the attention and enjoy whatever comes up … so to speak … that is, if you want to!"

Needless to say, this was a steep learning

curve for me to face and it took courage. And no, I'm not telling you how the evening ended! My point is, making changes, jumping into the unknown (or bed) can be challenging, and a really good thing ... maybe even fun. Sure, we make mistakes; that's how we grow. I might have been 44, but my ageless soul certainly felt a lot younger ... and quite possibly, acted it! I began to face, and deal with, my "new" reality.

Oh, and lest you think that I was just another party girl, my adventure into academia culminated with a BA in Journalism, after which I accepted a position teaching TV production at the University of Nevada-Reno. It also culminated with the end of my marriage ... all within a week. Talk about being reborn!

So, what do you want — or not want — in your life? Do you hate to go to work every day? Is it the job itself or the people you work with that make you miserable? Is there something else you've always wanted to try but felt you couldn't make a living or be successful at it?

Maybe you're in a relationship or marriage that's bereft of love, missing communication and affection, and lacks intimacy; you don't have much in common any more, but the mere thought of rocking the boat scares you half to death. You feel trapped, unable to make a change. You've accepted that this is how it will be, how you'll spend the rest of your life. It's called "emotional divorce."

You complain, commiserate, and share with friends. They listen and sympathize and some even empathize because they're in the same unstable boat. You want to make a change but you just can't. Believe me, I do know how you feel. All I'm asking you to do is think, to take a reality check on your world, your life.

Here's a good exercise that might help. Once again, honesty is key. Write down your goals for one year from now. How do you want to see your life at that time? Get in touch with your gut. How will you feel if your life remains exactly the way it is now? Are you depressed? Stomach in a knot? Or maybe your stomach's full of butterflies and you're feeling excited about the wonderful things you could be experiencing?

Now think about where you want to be in five years. Are you in the same job? With the same partner? Living in the same location? Feeling buried in the same old routine and bored out of your mind? Of course, life could deal us some cards we're not privy to at the moment that could change our direction. But aside from that, think about whether you can happily accept your life as it is at the moment … in five years. Nothing is too big or too small to consider. Do you want to have a great, fulfilling career, or be retired and living in the country? Travel the world, write a book, paint a picture? Do you want to be single or married?

This is the time to really daydream about possibilities. This is for *you*. Only you. Touch your heart at the deepest level. The person you are inside — your very soul — is the one who is most important. Let her shed tears of joy or grief, feel the pain if it's there, and write about it. Change cannot happen unless we're clear about what needs to be changed. Denial has no place here.

Making decisions, choices, can be so difficult, energy draining, frustrating and confusing! I once watched my son agonizing over whether to have a seafood omelet or a combo plate for lunch, and while I laughed at the difficulty he was having, the truth is, I have the same problem! He has trouble with most decisions. So do I … from deciding what I want to do with my life, down to what to wear to a party. The test is to make choices that answer the question — *what do I really want?*

To forego definitive choices makes you appear to lack "a mind of your own," wanting — perhaps needing — someone to tell you what to do. And by waiting for someone else to tell you what to do, you've given *your* power to them. That's demoralizing … and another chapter.

I needed to look at — and answer — the questions, *what do I really want to do?* And *what am I afraid of?* When I did, my mind threw up a barrage of obstacles, all the "what ifs." *What if* I do this and then don't like it? *What if* I'm not good at it? *What if* I can't make a living at it? All those *what ifs* can be very loud inside your head. But listen closely for the inner voice; the one shouting loudly, "Help me! I'm locked in!" Behind that door is independence.

There's little sadder than a decision made by indecision, also known as avoidance. The result of that is *not* living, not being truly involved in and enjoying life. Always being on the periphery just isn't fulfilling. It's holding back that piece that doesn't want to get hurt—self-protection that prevents vulnerability that prevents true depth of feeling. Some of us have been terribly disappointed and hurt in our lives to get to such an indifferent place, not always detached from others, but rather, from ourselves; well insulated from pain, but from our dreams and goals as well.

It's time, now, to make some decisions, to regain power, and take control of your life. Open the door and walk through it to find your dreams. Believe me; the rewards can be worth all the challenges. It's time to step out of your comfort zone because—let's face it—you really do have only one life to live. Throw out those fancy boots that don't fit and grab your running shoes. We're taking a journey starting right now!

moment for you to live, and that is the present moment."

Whatever happens, it happens for the best. Believe it or not—and Lord knows it's hard to believe sometimes—all the events in our lives are in our best interest and help to shape us into the human beings we are now, as of this moment, today. They are learning experiences, our own personal journeys, and although we may not understand the whys and wherefores at the time, if we pay attention, we'll eventually find the reasons and the value in those lessons. So let's be as grateful as we can be for our present circumstances, and especially grateful that those circumstances can be changed. That's what this book is about.

We were given life for many, many reasons— admittedly, the sperm and egg thing was major, but I'm looking for something deeper than that. We need to become aware of our challenges, whether or not we decide to overcome them. In fact, listing them is not only cathartic, but can also help us focus on what was important to our development. For now, let's limit the list to the "big" events.

Maybe you're overly shy, too abrasive, too stubborn, too selfish or too generous; perhaps it's a drinking or smoking problem, or you're an inveterate worrier or chronic procrastinator. Let your mind fly.

When the list is finished, go over it and be

discerning about what *really* should be there. You'll find that there may be items that are no longer beneficial or even pertinent to you. It's time to identify all the "mind clutter." By that I mean, the stuff that bogs you down when you dwell on it. That stuff you need to let go. Offload. Jettison. Sweep out. Release. Whatever your verb, whatever your image, know that it's an ongoing process; maybe even a way of life. (Yes, I still deal with this, too.)

How many times have you been chatting with friends and acquaintances and had the conversation turn to, "Well, when I was a little girl, I had to …" followed by someone jumping in with, "Oh! Me, too! In fact I did thus and so … ?" One by one, the talking stick is passed and everyone tries to top the last person's story. It's called living in the past. Yes, we are the result of our past, but none of us can change it! It's over! Done! Acknowledge it, let it go, and move on. And like any good move, some packing up is required, so fill that first box, and in a little while, we'll decide whether to chuck it into storage or leave it on the curb for trash pickup.

Trying to be the *me* I was in years past doesn't work. The junior prom queen tiara is packed away. (Well, I only bring it out when the French maid outfit is in the wash … !) To those around us, we are who we are right now—hopefully someone loving, caring, and reasonably happy and healthy.

If not, let's work on getting there.

Likewise, when I meet a mature person, I don't envision them as the cute or handsome teenager they probably were. Even with an old yearbook and sporting a letter sweater, I'll never know the person they were then. Of course, some of the "vintage models" may still act like silly kids at times, and that's often a really good thing.

I had back surgery a year ago, and my goal was to be able to jitterbug again. I am pleased to report that I now can and do! For the record, I don't care how that looks to anyone else because it puts a grin on my face and — or so I'm told — a twinkle in my eye.

I'm sitting here at the computer this morning, a product of past experiences, yes, but no longer defined by the girl I was 50 or 60 years ago. I'm a mother, wife, a sister, a friend and a grandmother. Those are just some of the roles I play, and underneath all of them, *I'm just me*. Going forward, I will continue to face challenges, trusting that those life lessons will be appropriate and adequate for my soul to learn all I need to know.

Does the word "guilt" mean anything to you? 'Cause anyone who doesn't have *some* sense of guilt hanging around somewhere is either a paragon of virtue or delusional. For example, have you said, "I should have ... Why didn't I? I wish I hadn't ... I wish I had ... They'll never forgive me for …," etc.? Guess what. That's just more useless baggage. What can you do about it? Pay more attention to your gut feelings so you don't do things you're going to regret. And yes, if you listen, you'll know. As for all those *should'a, could'a, would'a's?* Forget about them! What's done is done, so quit wasting your good energy on regrets. It just creates stress and fear, and ages us faster than just about anything else.

Here's another one: "I wish I'd spent more time with my children when they were growing up." Oh, how often I've heard that from both men and women. (If wishes were pennies, I'd be a rich woman … how about you?) All of a sudden, that cute little bundle of joy is 18 and on their own. Where did the time go? The fact is, under the circumstances that our parents faced and the ones *we* faced, we did the best we could at the time we did it. Sure, mistakes were made, but wallowing in guilt and regret isn't going to change a thing. So let it go and move on.

Please don't think that I'm recommending suppression of important and happy memories. They're part of that learning curve that helps us make better choices as we go through life. But there's a fine line between suppressing, stamping down, and burying, versus becoming aware, accepting, and then, letting go. It's like repacking some of those memories in a big box, taping the box up real tight, taking it to a storage unit, and locking it up … but keeping the key to the padlock on the door just in case. You don't need it cluttering your life at the moment, but you haven't buried it in an unmarked grave never to be found again either.

I'm going to go to *my* storage unit now and extract a small box as an example.

My first ten years of life had their challenges, but for the most part, I was pretty carefree and happy. Being an only child can be a lovely experience. It can also be lonely, especially when families with more kids come around, just oozing companionship and togetherness, and you suddenly realize just how insular your own little world really is. Heck, I had to call a friend (or invent one) just to play Hide and Seek! So I made use of every turkey wishbone, every candle on a birthday cake, and every first star at night to wish for a baby brother or sister. Then one day, Mom, who hadn't been quite herself lately — putting on a little weight and doing a lot of whispering with her friend — sat me down for a talk. She was smiling.

"Judy, your tenth birthday is coming soon. Would you like to have a party, or would you like to have a baby brother or sister for your present?"

"Oh Mom, do you mean it? Oh, yes! I want a baby to play with. When can we get it? Can we get it now?"

Remember, this was 1945. I had absolutely no clue where babies came from. My mother got "fat," but I truly didn't have any idea what was going on. Neither of my parents could have said the word "sex" out loud, let alone speak openly to their 10-year-old daughter about it—although obviously they knew more about it than they let on.

A few days after my tenth birthday, Mom went to the hospital. Ten days later (now it's 24 hours, if that!) my brother arrived home all bundled up in a blanket. He was just adorable. I was absolutely thrilled. Wow … a real live doll! I got to hold my very own sleeping baby. It was a Zen moment.

It was a really short-lived Zen moment. The reality was that my brother cried. A lot. He spit up. Often. And wow … he sure did smell. Really, *really* bad. He also got the lion's share of my mom's quiet, loving time while I got the crabby, short-tempered, sleep-deprived time. And when Dad came home from work, he focused on his new son so single-mindedly that I was left asking myself just what was so darn special about being a boy. Weren't girls good enough? So maybe *I* wasn't good enough? Disillusioned, rejected, sad, with a healthy dose of mad tossed in, three weeks passed.

"Mom, I've changed my mind. I really do want to have that party after all. Could you please take the baby back to the hospital?"

"I'm sorry, Judy, but he's ours now. I can't take him back. Do you want to hold him for a while?"

"No thanks, Mom. Please … can you just make him be quiet?"

It was a blow. Due to circumstances completely beyond my control, my life had changed forever. I might not have known the saying, "Be careful what you wish for because you just might get it," but I sure knew that I wasn't the center of attention anymore. We couldn't do all the fun things we'd done before, like climbing a mountain, being in stage plays with my mother, walking the mile to the library, or going to Maine.

And to top it all off, two months later, we uprooted from our lovely little home in Massachusetts, left my neighborhood friends and my fun and familiar grade school, and moved to a small town in New Hampshire. Dad might have had a better job, but I felt displaced on every level and utterly betrayed on several very important ones.

My point is that it was a tough time for me. Perhaps my parents could have handled it better, but they did the best they knew how at the time. I grew to love my brother dearly, and came to accept that none of this was his fault. He didn't choose to come into my world to make me miserable. I must say here that he was—and is—a gift from God, and I'm so glad they couldn't return him!

The move north was a fork in the road for all of us. Who knows what life would have been like if we'd remained in Framingham? I had many lessons to learn and I was given the opportunity to do so. Granted, I didn't understand that at the time, but those early challenges helped shape who I am today, and I'm pretty sure that's an okay person.

So my tenth birthday surprise changed my life and, yes, I've suffered some guilt over those early feelings. But the pain I felt as a result of those experiences is long gone, and I will now return that event and its Ghost of Guilts Past to the little box. It was important to me at the time—I own that—but I certainly don't need to keep it in my closet any longer!

I like to think of life's journey as a drive through the desert, appreciating the colors of the closest mountain range with its crags and valleys and outcroppings of rocks. It's like the first level of self-awareness. How proud we are that we "know" ourselves so well … each little flaw, each trauma overcome. Then we look beyond the first mountain to another range, a bit hazier, less defined, and realize there's another level of awareness to be investigated. More things, thoughts, feelings to be acknowledged. It just takes a little more work to see and know them, but it's necessary if we are to know ourselves. More mountains, more self-knowledge, other levels of insight—deeper, harder to see. And so it goes through as many layers and distances as it takes to reach the crisp, pure skyline where knowledge is infinite and the ranges of violet and purple and pink transition into clear blue sky that goes on forever.

It's work, too, this journey of ours. It's easier to just keep our eyes on the road and drive; get to our destination as fast as we can. But the beauty of looking around—looking further, deeper, closer—gives us an all-encompassing perspective of not just the world we live in, but of the internal/mental/spiritual world that is who we are as well. How dull the landscape would be without the depth of ridges, peaks, valleys and shadows.

Likewise, how uninteresting we would be if we continually looked at only one layer of consciousness without acknowledging the deeper levels of our souls. Even after years and years, we can still find our stash of old post cards from previous stops along our journey and pull them out to be examined, processed and mentally stored.

A friend told me about being home with his parents one day. It was crisp and clear and his father was chopping wood. When he was telling it, you could see that he was viewing the whole thing in his mind like a slide show. His father had paused between ax blows, looked directly at Steve and told him, "You'll remember this day. Everything about it."

For whatever reason, that had aggravated his mother. "Don't tell him that!" she'd said. But Steve did remember, and the day was carved crystal in his mind. His dad died of cancer, and a really nasty variety, so I've often wondered if perhaps his dad had just been diagnosed when that happened.

Take joy in the good memories. Cherish that first kiss, the highlights of accomplishments, the births of your babies, the accolades for work well done. Just don't live there. Shed some of that baggage to make room for the new. It's the first day of the rest of your life, so make it a good one.

It may help to create a ceremony — we humans have been doing it for years! Light a candle, share a meal, pour a cup of tea or glass of wine ... then burn your list, or bury it! Create a short mantra to accompany the process and end with a thank you to the Universe for your ability to let it go. Then drive on toward your new beginnings!

~THREE~

*"The fastest way to freedom is
to honor your feelings."*
Gita Bellin

They're Your Feelings—Honor Them!

Now that you're on your way, I'm willing to bet that if fear hasn't already raised its ugly head, it will somewhere along the way. And that's okay. Whether fear comes from *what might have happened if?* or *I knew he had a temper, but I didn't know he was dangerous,* or any of a lifetime's worth of events and relationships, let it rise to the surface and then treat it just like you treat that nasty yellow fat in a can of chicken soup. It won't kill you, but it's healthier to skim it off.

All feelings — good or bad — must be honored. You might feel defensive about your actions, but you never need to feel that way about your feelings. They're valid and they're yours. No one can *or should* argue with them.

Likewise, there are times when you just don't know how you feel. The situation can be as simple as deciding which restaurant you want to go to, or as complex as figuring out how much you love someone ... or even if. The first is a momentary puzzle of relatively little consequence, but the second? Yeah, that one may take some soul searching. I wish I could help you make such decisions, but I can't.

There are times when we want a friend, spouse or partner to be just a little dominant ... for instance, after a particularly long day, to be told, "Grab your coat, honey. We're going to the Pizza Piazza (or wherever) for a bite tonight." It's okay to say, "Sure ... good idea," and smile. Or not. Personally, there are times when I just want to be relieved of making a decision. It can feel comforting. And remember, it's always okay to "just say no." I truly hate conversations such as:

"Where would you like to go?"
"I don't know. Where would you like to go?"
"I don't care. Wherever you want to go is fine."
"Well, I don't care either!"

It can go on and on and the evening is ruined because nobody would make a decision. Been there, done that. We need to find the courage (spine) to express our feelings. Holding your tongue to keep the peace isn't worth the price — it can make you frustrated, bitter, and even worse, ill. (Hmmm. And I wondered why I developed back problems through the years! Duh ...)

Love, of course, is more complicated. I think those people who are bowled over with love at first sight are fortunate. It's a wonderful feeling to just know; one can only hope it's mutual! We'll get into relationships later.

Have you ever had a strong intuition hit in your heart, head or gut? Did you pay attention? Awareness is the first step; the second step is acting on it. Many years ago, my husband, Jim, and I had moved our company to Scottsdale and were trying to decide where we wanted to live; some place cooler, with mountains and pine trees. We studied maps, took road trips and explored all our possibilities.

We decided that Prescott was the answer to our needs. It was, and still is, a lovely town with a pleasing town park in the center. After devouring real estate fliers, newspaper ads, and covering every drivable street we could find, we were shown a new house in a development, all ready for final decisions on colors and upgrades. I wasn't overwhelmed with excitement, but it had everything we needed. It was … nice … suitable … okay.

We signed papers and headed back down the freeway to our temporary condo.

Within ten minutes, I had a knot the size of a volleyball in my stomach. Tears welled, escaped, sliding down my cheeks. Jim was alarmed because he had no idea what was wrong. Neither did I! By the time we reached the condo, I knew we'd made the wrong decision. I had no idea why. Logic wasn't part of it … just a deep inner feeling that I honored and, thank goodness, Jim respected.

Fortunately, the realtor was understanding and tore up the offer, and the powerful sense of relief I felt confirmed my feelings. We later found a lovely acre of land in Pine and built a house that we loved and planned to live in "forever." It was perfect … at the time. Another lesson learned. Nothing is forever …

Four years later, we were driving from Denver back to Pine and decided to spend the night in an off-the-main route dot on the map in southern Colorado. We'd never heard of it, but when we drove up the hill and saw the magnificent San Juan Mountains of Pagosa Springs, we looked at each other and said, "Whoops, we made a mistake. *This* is home!" The next day we were at a realtor's office, looking for land. No questions, no tummy knots, just that knowing for both of us.

We've been here sixteen amazing years now, and have so many dear friends. However, we know better than to say we're here "forever" — although we'd like to be.

"*Forever?*" said my cousin.

"*Maybe. But it's really too soon to tell.*"

Which is apparently, according to her, a

relative to:

"Live there all your life?"

"Not yet."

Thanks, Sam ...

What I do know, is that the older you get, the easier it seems to be to speak up about how you feel.

In some ways, the good little girl I was as a youngster — seen but not heard — took a long time to grow up. I learned the hard way that voicing your feelings could get you into a lot of trouble.

A quick example: I was around 12 at the time. We'd moved to New Hampshire and my brother was two. It's already been established that I wasn't overjoyed with the turn of events. I supposed it was a nice Sunday and my folks wanted to go for a drive. I didn't.

"I don't want to go. He gets car sick and I hate that. I won't go," I said with that defiant look on my face.

Dad, who I know with hindsight, had had about all he wanted with defiant children (vice principal of junior high at the time), gave me a quick little slap across my face. He had never done that kind of thing before, although he might have wanted to, nor did he ever do it again.

Needless to say, I got in the car. And needless to say, about an hour into the drive, my brother tossed his lunch, breakfast and probably last night's bottle all over him, me, and the backseat.

I may have won the point, but it was one horrible ride home.

(This *really* needs to be stored in one of my boxes with a key!) But as I said before, don't let anyone else tell you how you *should* feel about anything. The reverse, of course, respecting other people's feelings as well as your own, is also really important. Hurting someone else's feelings just so you can vent yours is unacceptable.

It bears repeating: *Feelings do not need to be defended.* Bad attitudes are not the issue here, but if your feelings are dishonored, then you'd better take a good look at the company you're keeping.

It's absolutely essential with a loved one, whether a mate, or child, or parent, or friend, to communicate feelings honestly. When the answer to "Are you alright?" or "What's wrong?" is a terse "I'm fine," walls go up. "Fine." What the heck does that mean? I really dislike that word.

I remember well when I started dating Jim. He would look deep in my eyes and ask, *"What's the matter?"*

"Nothing. I'm fine," I'd say, looking off to the side.

"I saw something go across your eyes. Tell me."

Good grief. No one had ever looked that deeply, carefully, caringly, into the real me before and my programming was, "I'm fine." Deny my feelings, suck it up, don't make waves ... the bottom line was that I didn't matter ... or that everyone else mattered more. Toss in a little fear of confrontation and there was Judy, lips tightly zipped. Of course something had crossed my mind, and yes, he'd seen it in my eyes — the eyes are the windows to the soul.

It was incredibly difficult and sometimes painful for me to open up and share, but with his encouragement, I slowly came to accept that the world wouldn't end, no matter what I said, and that he wouldn't let it go until I choked out whatever it was. He never gave up, and I learned to open up. He, laughing, might tell you he sometimes regretted it, but our love grew deeper with the shared communication. Feelings were honored. It took time. I liken it to slowly unzipping the protective suit I'd worn most of my life.

It's a pretty well known fact that many men are good at hiding their feelings, especially those raised by the John Wayne standard that it's unmanly to show hurt or sensitivity. The mere suggestion of a conversation about feelings — ours or theirs — and they clam up like a rock! For them, it's all about being a "big boy." Likewise, many girls are taught that "Big Girls Don't Cry." Great song. Lousy way to live.

I was the product of stalwart New Englanders,

and for years I thought of myself as "a strong woman." Being a mom tends to promote and even necessitate that particular image. Silly me. Just like the guys, I had fallen prey to the John Wayne School of Silent Macho ... keep a stiff upper lip, don't let them see you sweat, keep calm and carry on, and all the rest of those idiotic sayings which are only useful in idiotic situations. Like war. Thank goodness, I figured out that I was a work in progress and figured out that sensitivity and compassion in a partner are rare and wonderful gifts, beneficial to both parties.

It's a beautiful thing when a manly guy can allow his feminine side to emerge without shame. My husband has shared that gift with me. (I thank his mom for that.) As virile as any man I've ever met and definitely not lacking in testosterone, Jim chokes up at Hallmark commercials, Veteran's Day Parades and all manner of heart-warming events, including news stories. Our kids tease him, but it's a blessing beyond measure. He's not ashamed of his sensitivity and neither am I. He truly honors his feelings.

And that brings us back to fear, which often crops up when you're tiptoeing through territory where you feel vulnerable. First rule: Don't sabotage yourself. I hear all the what ifs out there. *What if I share my feelings and make someone mad? What if they leave me? What if I fall apart ... I'd be so embarrassed!*

Come on, girls! Get a grip! This is why you're reading this book. Just ask yourself, *What's the worst thing that can happen?* And when you have that worst thing in mind, then repeat after me, *So what?!*

If you're respecting your feelings, stating your case, and the reaction is negative, simply state, *This is how I feel.* Repeat as many times as you need to, and don't whine. If your partner can't or won't hear you, or it becomes apparent that your feelings mean nothing to them, then maybe it's time for you to get them out of your life or for you to get out of theirs. And as said before, what's the worst thing that can happen? Think about it.

We're fearful about so many things. It was about ten years ago when I was delivering copies of my first book, *EarthShift,* to our local book store/coffee shop. A stunning gal who was waiting behind me stepped forward and picked one up.

"Did you write this book?"

"Ah, yes, I did." I blushed, having no idea why she was asking.

"Well, I have this book and I loved it. Could I talk to you for a minute?"

"Um, yes, if you'd like." I was very new to the publishing world and had zero confidence in my ability. Introductions were made and we sat down

with our lattés.

"So," she continued, "I'm doing a yoga boot camp and I want you to come. It'll be for a week and all expenses will be paid."

"Sorry, I don't do yoga."

"You can learn it. I want an older woman in the group and you can talk about your book."

"But I'm really busy right now, and ... and ..."

"No buts. I'll send you the information. You'll have a good time."

And this insanely beautiful young woman with an amazing figure disappeared out the door, leaving a very flustered older woman in a state of shock. But I do believe in synchronicity, and I had been wondering how to market my book. My husband would be gone on a business trip at the time of the "boot camp" and I most definitely was not busy. So I took a chance. Here is what I wrote about it afterwards:

"I'm too old for that ... I'm hardly what you call a Goddess!" That was my reaction to being invited to attend a Yoga Boot Camp ... for Goddesses, no less! Friends and family did their best to instill some confidence in my wavering self-image. But I had the time open and soon began to think of it as a very real challenge to my fears about growing old. I decided to give it a go.

I collected the items on my list which included

army fatigue pants, tights (seriously?), and hiking boots, and nervously awaited the big day. With increasing trepidation, I drove up the long road and turned into a driveway which led to a beautiful mountain lodge nestled in a huge meadow with pine trees, a winding river, and a breathtaking view of the mountains.

Other attendees began to arrive from around the country. All 12 were very friendly and highly accomplished. And young. They could easily have been my granddaughters; all beautiful, talented, and did I mention young? So, so young. Again, I began to question why I was there and seriously considered making a fast getaway.

I'm pretty good about exercising, but Yoga was new. With the amazing backdrop of sky and mountains, our leader began to put us through our paces ... and parts of my body that I didn't know existed painfully awoke! We had Yoga sessions twice a day, and it was a stretch (pun intended) for me. The good news is that I managed to keep up ... not perfectly, but well enough to allow my ego to stay intact. Until the belly dancing, and I will freely admit that that left something to be desired, but we were all self-conscious and laughing so much it didn't matter.

I experienced my first Labyrinth by candlelight, made up my own special aromatherapy compounds and was amazed at how accurate the different decks *of inspirational cards were. I drew "Changing Woman," a pretty right-on description of what was happening.*

As the days went by, we became a close-knit group, and very supportive of each other. One of my biggest fears was the four-mile hike up a mountain trail and back. I have a bad knee and an arthritic foot. Having to quit part way up — or worse yet, not being able to walk down — was a frightening reality. Whether it was the adrenalin or conditioning from the week of training, I don't know, but I do know that I made it! Not only did I make it, I kept up with all those young, svelte women, and when we were done, I felt like a million bucks.

The most healing, wonderful experience for me came at the end when emotions surfaced and we shared our tears as each woman bared her soul. I'm a pretty controlled person and tend to keep my emotions to myself ... usually ... but when my time came to talk, the truth poured out of me along with the tears; the fear of not being able to keep up, of not being accepted because of my age, of not having anything in common. My new friends quickly assured me that I had no reason for any of my concerns. More tears and hugs and whatever lingering negative emotions were released. My feelings were honored. It was such a blessing and an incredible catharsis.

It was a week to remember. I made wonderful friends ... most importantly, I made friends with myself. Yes ... I think I feel like a real Goddess now!

Passion in your life—for your work or hobbies, nature, the ocean, the mountains, writing, painting, acting, theater, pole dancing or calf roping—passion is another thing that must be acknowledged. (Not sexual passion, mind you. That's tackled in another chapter. And don't go skipping ahead!) True happiness, emotional and spiritual fulfillment, and sometimes, even financial gain, can be had by following our passions.

It's likely you'll have more than one over the span of a lifetime, and it's wise not to bury them. You and I both know that it's way too easy to put your dreams on a back burner when we're stressed, overwhelmed, having to take responsibility for a hundred things at once. Or someone has convinced you that it's "not the thing to do" for whatever reason. However, once you can recognize what brings you joy, and feel your need and desire to experience it, there will be a way, and you *can* find it. It's called "manifesting." Look at J. K. Rowling. She hand-wrote the first Harry Potter book in a coffee shop in her spare moments. She had no money, just a huge dream.

I would suggest that you write a list of your passions, whether it's one or ten. It helps you focus. Some passions might be seasonal, or interrupted by a health issue or lack of finances, lack of time, lack of whatever, and need to be shelved for the time being. Beware the tendency to put off passion with excuses! But if you can home in on just one for now, and believe with all your heart that you deserve to have that in your life ... see it, feel it, intend to have it ... you might be amazed at what can happen. Thoughts are very energy-charged things. Just about everything in our lives is there because it was manifested, thought of, acted upon. Just bear in mind what Mom used to say, "Be careful what you wish for ..." and keep your thoughts positive and kind.

Once you make your list and have it whittled down, it's time to use discernment and have an inner conversation with yourself. *Why can I not do or have this in my life?* After you've hit the biggies, we'll get to the real roadblocks. Guilt was one of those for me. If something would feel that good, I probably didn't deserve it. So said my embattled self-image. There was so much more I "should" do, *had to do*, before allowing myself to fulfill my "selfish" desires. Just sit and read? No, no! I should be doing something productive.

I'm all too aware of the litanies of self-defeating excuses and reasons because I'm still guilty of making them. "Should" is a hateful word, and if you hear it often in your thoughts, then it's likely time to tell that nagging inner voice to back off. It's a sad state of affairs when the business of living gets in the way of life. But I'm getting better at recognizing my tendency to toss up my own roadblocks — and being aware is the big first step. Be true to yourself, trust your feelings, and honor yourself. Don't let anyone, with words or actions, diminish who you are ... ever!

Too many people face death aware that half their dreams remain unfulfilled because of the choices they made, and realizing, too, that they had alternatives.

~FOUR~

"If you wait, all that happens is that you get older."
Larry McMurtry, U.S. novelist

Making a Choice Isn't For Sissies!

You've come a long way … deciding if you want to make a change, defining your excess baggage, and getting started on lightening your load. Then you took an honest look at yourself, poked and prodded where the anger and judgment were hiding, and honored the feelings reeling around inside you. It's risky business, this digging down into your core and identifying our deep desires. So at this point, you might need a bit of bolstering up before you make some necessary choices. As the chapter heading says, it's not for sissies. But heck, growing old in general isn't for sissies, period!

It was once pointed out to me that since I played so many roles — wife, mother, sister, friend, daughter, etc. — I'd lost who I was … *my self.* The observation, both humorous and succinct, was, "So what role do you want to play, Judy? Keiser? Sesame? Onion? Don't define yourself as anything but yourself or you'll lose yourself and your own purpose." Talk about putting things into perspective! Sure, I was spread in all directions … it's just what we women tend to do! However, I'd left someone out. Me!

And now it's time for you. Will the real you please stand up?

One part of identifying ourselves is learning from our mistakes. Nobody's perfect, we all make them, and guess what? We're still here in spite of them. And small or large, they help shape who we are, even if we don't understand it until later. Hindsight being 20-20 and all. Often times, the mistake is made because we relied on someone else's well-meaning advice instead of listening to our own gut.

"How to Say No Without Feeling Guilty" is actually a class that I took when I went back to college years ago. It relates to the previous chapter on honoring yourself. Talk about anxiety!

The assignment seemed so simple — one week to find an occasion to say "no," and my kids and dog didn't count … damn. I had taken a newly purchased copper container to the florist and asked for a dried arrangement to be made. I described it … fall colors, earth tones, possible centerpiece. When I picked it up, I was so disappointed. It looked sparse and cheap — and it was. But the bill wasn't! I started to leave, stopped and reminded myself this was a perfect opportunity to stand up for myself. I took a deep breath and (shaking) went back and did my "no" thing. Much to my surprise, they agreed. I loved the replacement and after 30 odd years, still do. It's a great reminder.

So now it's time to reflect on your life again and find those things that gave you that "Yes I Can!" feeling—fears overcome, the sense of joy and pride that came with an achievement, the inner and outer pats on the back for standing up for yourself. Seek out the things that have nurtured your soul.

I'm bringing out one of my *ah-ha* experiences from storage to share. It's a choice that has helped me many times since. It was a few years after my first son was born and I was desperately trying to get pregnant again. Lots of counting days, taking temperatures, the pain of yet another period appearing that would send me into tears. After suffering a miscarriage, the doctor suggested I get out of the house and get involved in something to take my mind off it all.

I joined the local little theater. As shy as I was, playing a role as someone else on stage had come quite easily to me in high school and college. Now though, it seemed like a big step. I auditioned, won parts, loved it, got pregnant and had my second son. And as soon as I could, I returned to the theater.

My acting highlight came when I was asked to play the part of Mrs. Manningham in *Angel Street,* a role made famous by Ingrid Bergman in the original movie, *Gaslight.* I would be on stage for the whole play and would need an English accent.

"I simply can't do it. I'd never be able to learn all the lines! And I don't have an accent!"

"We have faith in you, Judy. We'll help you. We know you can do it ... and we have a terrific leading man for you. Come on! Give it a try."

"But what about my babies and my husband!"

"It's only three rehearsals a week for six weeks."

"Well ... I'd really like to do it ... but let me check with my husband."

What was I saying!? But I made the choice. With a litany of prayers and promises, I began rehearsals. It wasn't easy. I lived, ate, and breathed the role. The director found a real, live person from England to help with the accent, the costume committee designed and made a great gown for me, sets were built and the days flew by. It was a massive undertaking for all of us. I was extremely nervous, but I had committed.

It's a very dramatic role. Bella's husband

tries to drive her insane by sneaking into the attic and lowering the gaslights every night. He hides things, then accuses her of taking them, then "finds" the items in her work basket. It works until a kindly detective, Joseph Cotten in the movie, recognizes the nefarious deeds. In the last scene, Bella still isn't totally sure her husband is guilty, and by this time, the audience is on edge. After a powerfully dramatic confrontation between the Manninghams, Detective Rough drags the evil husband out the door and sends him off to jail with two Bobbies as Bella sinks down in a chair.

"I'm so sorry for putting you through this, Mrs. Manningham. This has been a terrible night for you."

Slowly standing up and looking at the audience, I said the final line in my best Ingrid Bergman voice.

"Oh no, sir. This has been the best night of my life!"

We received standing ovations every night, rave reviews, and a number of people actually asked where I was from in England. In the end, my husband was *not* overjoyed, but it was still a perfect "Yes, I can" moment—one of the best choices of my life. I can still bring to mind the indescribable high of the experience and get goose bumps. I guess that means something! It was a huge step forward for my self-esteem.

Part of the take-away lesson for me was that I really could act. Heaven forbid I would ever have to stand up and just be me, Judy, in front of an audience, though. I used the lesson many years later when I took classes at the University of Nevada-Reno. It was fun being on a campus again. I majored in journalism, but when I went to the department library the first time, I was paralyzed with fear. Standing in the doorway, I decided to play the role of a TV reporter. I walked in with the confidence of one ... and it worked. By the time I graduated, I was *me*, just me. Graduation was, by the way, another "Yes I Can" achievement.

There are no limits except those we create through doubt and fear, and it's all too easy to give our power away. I was a master at it. I certainly deferred without a peep to my parents. And since I didn't have any realization, let alone appreciation, of my so-called power, I progressed into a marriage where I continued to give my power to my husband because it was expected. It was how things worked ... the thing to do. My power wasn't taken—I just surrendered it.

Look at it this way. If you feel that you need to take your power back, ask yourself "Back from what? Back from whom?" We have always had "the power." Nobody took it away. We gave it freely, especially in the '50s, but at other times, too, or in certain circumstances, most often unknowingly. But it's our choice, like it or not. Nobody else owns it. It's still ours and we simply need to find it again as it waits right inside ourselves.

It took many years for me to find my own *self*, to learn that I was somebody in my own right, and then to reach deep within and pull out the strength and awareness that allowed me to trust in *me*. That trust allowed me to become a woman who could stand on her own two feet and face the world straight on. Roar or not, I was WOMAN. I had found my own power and it rocked!

I learned another important lesson, too. You can't change someone else unless they want to change. You can only change your attitude about them. That's true for anyone, friends or partners.

As you might imagine, that much self-awareness didn't make for smooth sailing in a twenty-year marriage, especially one that had never been rocked, let alone sailed over rough water. However, it was my boat now and I was at the helm, steering *my* course.

We all walk in our own shoes and mine were getting more comfortable all the time. What I want to share with you is the knowledge that it's never too late, and we're never too old to make choices. We all face many forks in the road of our lives. We question our decisions and ponder what might have happened *if* ... just what *if* ... ? Richard Bach even wrote a book called *One* exploring the notion of parallel — but differently chosen — lives.

But you know ... with my own 20-20 hindsight, I wouldn't change a thing. All my choices have led me to right here, sitting in my office and looking out the window at an incredible view of the mountains and the lake, married to a man I love deeply and who loves me back the same way. And our choices together have been really, really good. It works — and it's never too late for ah-ha moments!

~FIVE~

*"For those who believe, no proof is necessary.
For those who don't believe, no proof is possible."*
                                    Stuart Chase

Manifesting and Miracles

Conscious manifesting—the amazing ability we have that allows us to create our own reality—can and does produce miracles. We all manifest, all the time, with both good and bad results. But often, we're unaware of having done it. Things just … happen. Things we think or talk about—that parking spot just when you need one, a friend you were missing and just *happen* to run into at the store, the twenty dollar bill you find in the couch when you're simply too tired to cook.

Or perhaps it's the fulfillment of a desire hidden so deep inside that you weren't even aware of it. But once it happens, you can't help wondering why the dickens you didn't do it, buy it or go there years before. We call it coincidence, serendipity or luck, referring to things, people and events whose orbits cross the paths of our lives and leave us saying, "Well, I'll be damned!"

Allow yourself to consider what could happen if you capture that ability and work it. I'm not talking about greed here. Meditating on Power Ball numbers or the stock market isn't where we're heading. I'm talking about creating more of what you desire in *your* world, *your* life. *The Secret,* by Rhonda Byrne, was one of the first mainstream books to address this possibility.

If you're not aware of the option—and power—of creating, then your thoughts could also be instrumental in bringing negative experiences to you. As I've said before, I'm a firm believer that what you think about is what you get.

Perhaps you've heard yourself mumbling, "I can never remember names." Guess what? You never will, unless and until you change your affirmation to something positive. And yes, if you always say this when a name doesn't immediately come to mind, believe me, it's an affirmation! I know, because I haven't spent enough time on this one, either!

Of course, the belief that you can, in fact, change a thought pattern must be there. That's where the need for intention comes in. Your desire must be firmly rooted in the belief that you *can* accomplish a change by changing your thoughts, and accept as fact that the process works. Believing is seeing.

The phrase "I can't" is one of the most deadly

of all phrases. It's a great way to slam the door shut on any help that your angels might be able to give to you. Changing your thoughts from "I can't" to "I can, I will, I am" allows the "Universe" to begin paving the way towards making it— whatever wonderful thing "it" is—happen. Another stumbling block is expecting immediate gratification and not getting it, immediately giving up, then proclaiming loudly, "See? It doesn't work." There's a reason that patience is a virtue.

Your particular goal may require multiple steps; think of it as crossing a stream on stepping-stones. Sometimes, you jump ahead. Sometimes you jump to the side. Sometimes you just jump, and trust that the stone you're aiming for isn't quite as far away as it looks! The stones are there, our gifts to give us guidance. Concentrate on those, ignore the depth of the water and those nasty fear-fishes swimming in it. Keep your eyes on the stones, take the leaps—yes, *of faith!*—and reach your goal.

Your steps might be meeting someone who mentions a class or recommends a book to you. It sounds interesting … appealing, and it happens to be exactly what you need at that moment. Or perhaps an unexpected check arrives in the mail at just the right amount, or a friend calls and invites you to go somewhere and that leads to something, or maybe even something magical.

The possibilities are endless.

The point is, our higher beings see the overall picture and have the means to help us through our streams, step by step. Quite simply, if we express our desire with passion and the absolute knowing that we can reach the goal, we will. I call it *going with the flow*. The phrase "Living in the Now" also fits. It's important to remember that our stones become difficult, if not impossible, to see if you lose your trust and belief in the system.

My very first manifestation done with total awareness occurred many years ago. (Obviously, I had manifested many things in my life prior to that, both good and bad ... just not on purpose!) On a flight to Vegas to do a show, a magazine tucked into the seat pocket caught my eye. *New Woman*. Talk about appealing! I started thumbing through it and found an article on affirmations by Shakti Gawain that looked interesting and seemed to address the situation I was dealing with at that time ... mainly, a desire to change my life. As you might expect, my emotions were in turmoil. I was frustrated in both my work and my relationship, and at a complete loss to know what to do about either. (One of her books is called *Creative Visualization*.)

Following Gawain's instructions, I composed two sentences, an affirmation of what I wanted in my life, and wrote them twenty times a day. The most difficult part for me was truly believing in the process; accepting that those things I was affirming had already happened in my life. My affirmation went something like this: "*I am happy, healthy and strong. I am successful in my work and fulfilled financially, and my love life is perfect.*" I felt like a complete fraud stating those things, saying my affirmation in the present tense while "knowing" that I was asking for things that seemed impossible at the time.

It took a few days to get my mind wrapped around the concept. The total involvement of my senses … physically writing the words, seeing the words, reading them aloud as I wrote, and believing with all my heart that if I performed the exercise, I would have results. It was powerful. I usually did this just before bed so the thoughts would be on my mind during the night.

What happened you ask? Well, two weeks later, I was offered a three-month gig as the booth production assistant for the NCAA television football series. We traveled around the country for two games a week, and I met and worked with wonderful people who became a temporary family. I loved the freedom and the fun, and I gained self-esteem, self-confidence, and acceptance from my peers. Being on the road gave both my partner and me the space to step back from the relationship and reevaluate how we really felt.

That experience, that realization and manifestation of what were undeniably *my* deepest and most honest wishes and desires, gave me my "ah-ha" moment—awareness of what I could accomplish. I had really done it! Created my desired reality. Guided to the magazine article by unseen forces, I had followed my stepping-stones into the stream and across. It's easy to forget, or deny, that we have this power. I certainly did. At times, I still forget. What I don't forget is to acknowledge the guidance with thanks, whether the results of the process are large or small. This is very important, and perhaps why "saying grace" has been in practice for so long.

Let's face it ... we're all slaves to our habits; they're ours and we're used to them. Ruts? Sure... but *our* ruts. The unfortunate thing is that some of our habits are bad ones. In addition, what we think, say, do, and allow ourselves to hear continues, day in and day out, deepening those ruts until we accept them as unchangeable. In case you missed the memo: By perpetuating negative thought patterns, you condemn yourself to manifesting nasty, negative stuff. Thought = Cause. Result = Effect. Simple, right?

To quote "Abraham," a wonderful spirit who speaks through Esther Hicks:

"When people ask us how long does it take for

something to manifest, we say, 'It takes as long as it takes you to release the resistance. Could be 30 years, could be 40 years, could be 50 years, could be a week. Could be tomorrow afternoon.'"

http://www.abraham-hicks.com

How many times have you said, "I'll never be able to do that!" Or, "I can't climb that mountain," "I can't dance," "I'll never be able to swim," "I can't spell"? Choose your own "I can't _____" and fill in the blank. Or better yet, DON'T! Our subconscious minds take our statements as truth and follow our "orders" keeping us from achieving our "I can" in any way we can.

Let's change the thought to the positive. "I *want* to dance. I *will* learn to dance. I *can* dance … *I am dancing!*" And remembering to keep it in the present tense. By stating positives, we open those doors and allow ourselves to accomplish our goals. The effect of such positive thoughts *will* manifest. In all ways, we can break old habits and create peace, happiness, success, and good health in our lives. We *have* all those things *now!* It could be — can be — IS as simple as that. We just have to ask and believe … and that is the miracle.

I would be remiss not to caution you once more. The old saw goes, "Be careful what you wish for. You just might get it." I know I'm repeating myself, but thoughts are such powerful things. For instance, if you say, "I'm tired of working. I'd like to stay home for three months," you might find yourself physically unable to work—sick, or the victim of a car crash, or who knows what. You will have manifested your thought, but not the way you would have liked if you'd really thought about it. So be sure to monitor your thoughts carefully and send their energy in positive directions.

If, for instance, you are asking for good health, the stepping-stones might include a referral to a doctor or healer who can help you. They might in turn recommend doing something such as changing your diet or seeing another therapist. The steps are seldom in a straight line, but with the knowing, the belief, the trust and faith that your goal can be accomplished, it will be.

By 1987, I knew the process pretty well. Jim and I had married and moved into the country north of Los Angeles. Our home sat on two acres of land in a quiet little town. I had quit my job in the city because I had absolutely had it with the long commute in LA's impossible traffic, morning and night. We had started our own company, operated out of our home, and had decided that it was time for a pet to make everything perfect.

We decided on a Golden Retriever, searched for a litter, and through a series of coincidences, we found the perfect pup. She was the runt of the litter with big brown eyes and a happy smile. Home she came.

Sammy became totally integrated into our lives. She slept at my feet while I worked at the desk. We walked, hiked, talked, went to training school. It became apparent that she thought of herself as a human being, and was very unsure what those *other* four-legged animals were all about. At eight months, we decided that Sammy needed a furry buddy with a good personality, one that wouldn't de-throne her, but could hold his or her own. When the local pound didn't have anything to offer, I remembered the power of affirmations.

"We need ... no ... we <u>have</u> a dog for Sam to play with, a companion who's teaching her how to be a dog." Twenty times a day with all my heart poured into it, I wrote it, spoke it, felt it. It didn't take long to manifest, but in a way I couldn't possibly have imagined, and to this day, still find almost impossible to believe.

As I sat at my desk with a view across the valley, I noticed a car driving up the hill about a half mile away. It pulled off to the side of the road and someone got out. A small animal did, too. Then, although it took me a few minutes to register what was happening, the person got back in the car and drove away. The little creature tried desperately to catch up, tearing after the car as it sped down the main road and disappeared. Whatever it was, it had been dumped — left on purpose!

I ran out and jumped in my own car to see if I could find the critter. I could at least take it to the pound rather than having it be run over or starve to death. I had gone about 100 feet when this ball of hair came racing up the hill straight at me. I stopped, opened the door and said, "Hi. Who are you?" No collar and no tags. He wiggled and waggled and jumped right in. His hair was four inches long, matted and smelly. I had no idea what was under all that mess, but whatever it was, it was certainly amiable.

After a very wet (me as much as him) session in the bathtub, a brushing and some food, he began to stake his claim by lifting his leg on the furniture. "Oh, oh," said I. "This will never do. If you want to visit for a day or so, fine, but that kind of action must stop immediately, buster." And that is how Buster got his name.

During housebreaking, one strives to get the dog to the designated spot before they start to go. But it was impossible to tell with Buster! He was some sort of cross between a Poodle and a Lhasa Apso; heftier than either one, and with short legs and so much hair, you couldn't even tell when the leg went up!

Sam was fascinated. And timid. They sort

of tested the waters with each other. With her size and strength, she could move him around at will, even sit on him, but his deep growls let her know when enough was enough. He began exploring the property and she tagged along, something she had never done on her own. Sam was the proverbial little kid with her first friend.

Within a few days, it was apparent that Buster was becoming part of our lives, so we made a trip to the vet for shots. The vet guessed his age to be about eight months and deemed him to be in good health. That sounded just fine to me! After a trip to the groomer, I could finally see those big beautiful brown eyes, so full of love and gratitude. He was my miracle.

He was Sam's, too ... for the most part. You see, Buster quickly learned how much fun it was to entice the Golden to chase him through the house, but it was the difference between a thoroughbred and a quarter horse. Smaller and more agile, Buster would turn on a dime and run under the pool table where he'd sit and wait. Sam, going full tilt, invariably forgot to duck.

The affirmations had worked perfectly. Perhaps another person's prayers were answered, someone who couldn't keep a dog for some reason—possibly because the dog marked anything over two inches tall. It's terribly wrong to drop off a helpless pet in the middle of nowhere, but there's no doubt in my mind it was meant to be. Buster was with us for 16 years. And yes, was housebroken!

But enough of *my* stories. What would you like to manifest in your life? Narrow it down to just one item for now. You might want to start with something small so you can gain confidence in the method. Be careful of the wording as I said before. Put it in the framework that whatever it is, it's already yours. A done deal. Write it up! In present tense! Leave the details to the universe. Trust that it will find the right and perfect way to bring your miracle into your life. And be patient. Just know. Have faith. And remember to give thanks when they're due. Miracles do happen.

We were all born with a wonderful sense of inner knowing. Intuition. As adults, we sometimes know who's calling before answering the phone. Sometimes we get that gut feeling, perhaps even a warning, even though we don't always listen to it. It might be a tingle up the spine or goose bumps, or "just a hunch." Learn to trust it. Play with it. That awareness can be a lifesaver. It really does get easier and easier in time, and works better and better with practice.

It's good to take your intuition out in nature, too. There's even a whole new school of thought about the necessity of staying connected to the earth, as in barefoot ... on the dirt ... *grounding* ourselves, if you will. Grounding kits, sheets and silver wires aside, I do know that getting out to smell the grass and trees, watch puffy clouds drift by as they merge making pictures in the sky, makes me feel wonderful. Get out and listen to the sounds of the birds or the wind or even traffic. It focuses us. Be aware that it's your life speaking to you. Do you hear it? What's it whispering?

There have been times when I've told an intuitive hit to just back off; that I know what I'm doing. What happened? Well, unfortunately, when I chose not to listen, I'd inevitably take the wrong fork in the road and regret it. But we do learn from mistakes, thank goodness!

Meditation can, of course, be hugely beneficial with all this. It might be simply walking, sitting on a stump, climbing a mountain, listening to music, or perhaps taking deep breaths and clearing your mind. Yes, clearing your mind—an enormous undertaking sometimes! It takes practice. I know. However, it will open your mind to messages you might otherwise miss.

It's my opinion that with the energy shifts now happening, tuning in is getting easier and easier. Remember, it's never too late and you're never too old!

~SIX~

*"Inside every seventy-year-old is a
thirty-five-year-old asking, 'What happened?'"*
Ann Landers

Polka Dots and Cellulite

Out of the mouths of babes! My granddaughter was "helping" me find the letters on my computer and her observation caught me by surprise.

"Grammy! You've got polka dots on your hands!"

What a charming way to describe age spots! I laughed, told her she was right, and explained that that sort of thing usually happens when you get older. She asked a few more questions, and after my first gulp, I soon realized that it was fairly easy to explain aging to a four-year-old.

I also realized that my Mother really did know best — about so many things — but I didn't listen. Here are just a few:

1. It's important to honor your body. Sure, these days we can replace more parts when they

wear out, but that's not something most folks plan on or look forward to doing. Awareness of health options is much better nowadays than back in the 50s regarding maintenance and well-being of our bodies.

Nowadays, our options are expanding from conventional medical treatments with osteopathic and chiropractic therapy, and the occasional acupuncturist or masseuse, to include many newer — or is that older — alternative therapies. There's homeopathy, naturopathy, hypnotherapy, reflexology, traditional Chinese, Ayurvedic (linked to Buddhism and Hinduism), aroma therapy, juicing, herbal, diet and vitamin therapies, a range of energy therapies based on electricity, magnetism, and of course, simple prayer. The good news is that at least some mainstream doctors are more open to them.

In my day — and that is truly an ugly phrase, so let me rephrase — *in my early years,* options such as chiropractors, hypnotherapists, massage therapists, nutritionists, and naturopaths were few and far between. Smoking was considered cool. We buttered our burns, basted our skins until skin cancers popped up like chicken timers, and we allowed ourselves to be convinced that Wonder Bread grew healthy bodies 8 ways (12 ways by the 1960's) because of its "added nutrients."

We completely forgot the reason those

nutrients were added. Thanks to a government-sponsored program in the 1940's, they were to reduce the incidence of beriberi and pellagra caused by the white bread we were eating! The program worked and became known as "The Quiet Miracle," and it's only taken us how long to realize that whole grains bread is healthier? (The exception is if you're sensitive to gluten, and that takes a conversation with your doctor!)

Exercise consisted of walking to and from school (five miles, through rain and snow, uphill both ways!), riding bikes, jumping rope, ball games and whatever else we could enjoy on the playground. No wonder gym class was only once a week. Everything was safe, or at least seemed safer, even without helmets and the Consumer Product Safety Commission. We had no idea what a television set was, let alone video games, and that's the good and the bad of it.

It's very easy, in your 20s and 30s and listening to Bob Dylan, to think of yourself as "forever young," but that's not the way it works. When I was a kid, my aunts and grandmothers were heavy, happy women who wore big old Doctor Leonard's clunky, pliable, and comfortable, though not very pretty, shoes. They also wore girdles, flowered housedresses, aprons with big pockets, and had their gray hair permed and curled tight or pulled straight back in a bun. That's just the way it was.

I loved my aunts and grandmothers dearly, but aspire to any parts of their appearances? I don't think so! My mom refused to subject herself to the constraints of a girdle but bound her boobs flat because they were, at the time, considered too big! And let me tell you, breaking down that tissue does not bode well for staying perky as the years go by.

Times and opinions sure have changed about how long we can or *should* try to look young … or at least younger. But here's the catch. That tanned skin, well oiled and baked to perfection as a teen might look and even feel healthy then, but mother was right … skin deteriorates. In addition to those aforementioned polka dots, overexposure to the sun also develops wrinkles, and, more and more often, skin cancer when the years—and burns—pile up. So check out the new "tans in a bottle" that are by far easier and healthier than the bake, burn, and peel routine of yesteryear. It only takes one sunburn before the age of sixteen to increase your chance of developing melanoma by fifty percent. So anytime you must be in the sun, use your sunscreen. Please!

Connected to sun damage or perhaps just an aging result, you will have barnacles. That's what those little dry bumps that can appear anywhere, often behind the knees, on our arms and legs, are called. I knew I had them but only recently found out their name. Now I won't think of those cut-your-feet growths glued to rocks at the ocean the same way!

Cellulite: another one of those "what-the-heck-is-that?" features of aging. Whatever you do, don't — DO NOT — try on bathing suits in dressing rooms with mirrors. And that's really all I have to say about that.

Remembering Grammy's Doc Leonard shoes, I must say that whoever said, "When your feet hurt, *everything* hurts" was very, very wise. I wince in pain when I see women of any age scrunch their feet into three, four or even five-inch spike-heeled pointy-toed shoes. Oh yes, they make the calves look shapely and the legs look long. I wore pointed-toe shoes in the 50's, too, but with shorter heels. Arthritic joints now make it clear that even lower heels might not have been such a good choice. Just remember, if you're not careful, your hard-working feet, abused and taken for granted, will someday show signs of all that wear and tear. Joints will swell, toes curl under, hammertoes might develop, and instead of wearing those sexy, dainty size 7's, you'll still be in agony even when your toes are splayed out in a size 9.

And really, ladies, there *are* attractive shoes out there, a wide variety to choose from. In a time when *haute couture* includes everything from L.L. Bean boots to flip-flops, it's certainly possible to find a healthier compromise for style and comfort. All I'm saying is, please don't squeeze your feet into shoes that are too small or too high, and do wear something with support so your arches can live long, happy and nicely curved lives. There's no foot transplant yet, so those babies are all you have. Be nice to them. I sure wish I had been!

In addition, while we're talking about bones ... the toe bone's connected to the foot bone, the foot bone's connected to the anklebone, the ankle ... Okay, I'll spare you the rest of the trip up to the back and just say, *whatever you do, stand up straight!* Learn good posture when you're young and work on it in your later years. It helps you look confident and proud. Hold your head up, keep your shoulders down and back, and tuck in your tummy—sometimes described as "belly button to the backbone." Be proud of your "girls," big or small. Let them do whatever nature intended.

I have a strong memory of something that happened when I was about 3 years old. My nursery school teacher was dropping me off at home. Mom was there ...

"Sally," said my teacher, "Judy is only three and she's taller than all the other children. We'll just have to put a brick on her head!"

Yes, I was tall for my age from the moment I was born ... 22 inches and 5 lbs. I'm told Dad thought I looked like a monkey, but Gram stepped up to the plate and pointed out that I had straight eyebrows and a short upper lip and that I'd be beautiful. Bless her heart. Mom swore I'd been stretched out full length for the last three months of her pregnancy.

Anyway, although the teacher's comment was said in jest, it burrowed deep into my cell memory … an awareness that it was somehow bad to be tall. My shoulders drooped. I wanted to shrink, and tried every way I could to be shorter than the boys after I hit 5'8" in the sixth grade. I didn't have a chance in dance class. All I wanted was to be shorter.

My slouch even caught the attention of my 8th grade history teacher, who would walk up the aisle and tap me on the back with her ruler. "Sit up straight, Judy." Yeah, right … besides my height, I was also trying to hide the fact that I didn't have any boobs. Until college, when I discovered that Kotex could serve multiple purposes, it never occurred to me to pad my bras.

It took me a while to figure out that my teacher was right; when you're slumped over, you look like a loser with no confidence in yourself. With good posture, even a short person has stature. Thank goodness, the females these days are being encouraged to stand tall. Be proud of whatever height you are. You'll be perceived — and you'll perceive yourself—in a much better light.

Between poor posture, an inherited dowager's hump (thanks Mom) and a mild scoliosis (thanks Dad) I'm now 5'5" and holding. Shrinkage happens mostly in the spine and my waist has gone from being short to ... well ... non-existent!

I won't dwell on all the implications of having a "weak spine," but last year I had to have back surgery for Spondilolisthesis; technically, the L4 and L5 vertebrae had slipped over each other about a half inch. So now, I have my wish—I'm not only shorter, but I now have enough hardware to set off alarms at the airport! Every time I pull out the step stool to fetch something off a high shelf, I mourn those lost inches just a little.

The toll of time, gravity, heredity, and even lack of nutrition eventually catches up with us, like it or not, and regular exercise is the best thing you can do for yourself, no matter how old you are. Not only can weight-bearing routines build bone and ward off frailty, but running, jogging, walking, biking or swimming can protect against heart disease, diabetes, high blood pressure, colon cancer, depression, *and* exercise eases tension and reduces stress!

This is beginning to sound like way too much of a lecture, but before we move on, there's one more tremendously important key to long life and aging well. Please. Don't. Smoke. Nicotine is more addictive than heroin. Even one cigarette and you may be hooked. Besides all the health issues like lung and other cancers, emphysema and other lung diseases, heart disease and stroke, smoking creates those nasty little pucker lines around your mouth, and lipstick runs into those suckers like rain water into a stream. My husband and I both quit on May 24, 1984. I remember it well and will tell you truthfully, that it was *not* easy. Smoking is a nasty, smelly and expensive habit, and these days, it can turn you into an outcast. So before you start lighting up, picture yourself enjoying your coffee breaks standing the requisite 50 feet from the building, smoking all by yourself in the rain.

Another of the Ten Commandments of Clean Living (that's like The Body List's Bill of Rights) is to limit your intake of sugar, caffeine and alcohol. I see no reason to give them up completely unless you have a health issue and your doctor has advised it. Moderation is the key. Personally, I enjoy an evening cocktail or glass of wine with my husband. It's almost a ritual. But coffee gives me the jitters, so whatever caffeine I get is in the form of dark chocolate (which rates its own food group). I do occasionally enjoy a decaffeinated coffee latté with skim milk and whipped cream on top. Don't ask ... makes no sense, but it sure is good.

There are dozens of books and tapes and TV shows on diet and exercise written by wiser folks than I. Like the common cold, dieting and exercising have different requirements for all of us, and it's likely that bits and pieces of many programs and regimens will have benefits if applied. Personally, I love Dr. Oz and Dr. Weil. What a gift they are to the human race. I take some vitamins, including C and D3. And water … remember to drink plenty of it!

Doctors say we should get lots of sleep. Sounds like a plan to me, but sometimes easier said than done. It gets easier as your affirmations kick in and old baggage is tossed out.

Remember to smile and laugh more. It's contagious, and those laugh lines are the ones you want.

Take good care of your teeth and gums. Brushing and flossing are so important, even though dentistry has improved over the years. Thank goodness for that! I remember being given little silver mercury balls to roll around in my palms, a treat after enduring painful, no-Novocain drilling back in the day. I cringe at that memory for so many reasons.

Not done yet, but here's some good news: The hair in your armpits gets sparser and sparser. The bad news is that it migrates to your chin, and I can tell you, that's a nuisance! Just try catching those little suckers if your hand shakes at all.

So far, I've skipped happily over weight

gain, but I can't, in good conscience, ignore it. I've learned two things for sure. My doctor once told me that the norm is to gain 10 pounds a decade after age 50. Who me? Never! Well, the first ten just appeared unannounced, and the second ten has made inroads and is begging to be let loose. It is a struggle. The mere smell of a loaf of fresh bread can add a pound. Unfortunately, I love bread. And crackers and cheese. And fries. And … well, you see the problem here. Will power? Ha! That disappears faster than the hair in your armpits. The real crusher is the cold hard fact that often, as we age, we become more limited in how much and what kind of exercise we can employ to help burn those extra calories.

Almost done. Just one more item on the Body List, and it's an important one. Enjoy great sex, and choose your partner well. You're never too old and it's never too late. We'll explore this subject in greater depth in the next chapter since I've found that sex is *not* something "mother knew best" about. It was, sadly, never a part of our conversation.

And remember, not everyone has all these body issues, but as sure as death and taxes, those polka dots are going to show up sooner or later!

~SEVEN~

"It's ill-becoming for an old broad to sing about how bad she wants it. But occasionally we do."
Lena Horne

Afternoon Delight!

The heart, the mind and the soul long for it as we age, but the body doesn't always comply the way it once did. Neither does his. What is it? Sex, of course! The most intimate experience two people can share is the delightful act of making love.

Whether you're intimate with someone, lie with them, sleep with them, or know them Biblically; whether you have coitus, intercourse, or sex; whether you make love, make whoopee or go all the way; it's all natural and wonderful and best approached with a sense of humor! I give you those immortal words from that memorable chick flick, *Dirty Dancing*, "Oh, come on, ladies! God wouldn'a'given you maracas if he didn't want you to shake 'em!"

Physical intimacy means many different

things to men and women, and whether it's the full-on naked samba or just cuddling, to the majority of us, it's darned important no matter what our age. Sexual intimacy is often the barometer of the health of the relationship between two people. If it's not good in bed for either of you, and not something that can be resolved with compromise, there's probably something else going on that needs to be addressed. It's been said that sex — quality of it, quantity of it, pursuit of it — is the number one cause of a partner (men or women) straying. So just like our bodies, we need to take care of our relationships, too.

For eons, a double standard has prevailed in the "taking care of" department. Many little babies were and continue to be conceived due to the shortage of blood experienced within the male brain after arousal has pumped it south into his … shall we say, "lower extremities?" Call it passion, call it testosterone poisoning, call it whatever you want; a guy's instinct is to throw caution to the wind in pursuit of the almighty orgasm.

Females, on the other hand, even in the throes of raging hormones and an aching need to be held and loved, and yes, even *ravished*, tend toward perfect recall about the fact that they could become pregnant if precautions aren't taken (and I'm not even touching on STDs here!). So if becoming parents isn't part of everyone's plan, the situation is rife with challenge for both partners, but most especially for the prospective mother.

I haven't met a man yet who has carried a baby inside his body for nine months, dealt with morning sickness, survived delivery, not to mention breast-feeding for months. Birth control has changed the responsibilities to some degree, but a woman's take on sex was and is, without question, different.

Abortion, even when medically necessary, safe and available, is a traumatic event, and giving up a baby for adoption is wrenchingly painful, too.

Let me just say that if a baby is desired, being a mom and experiencing all the joys of feeling a baby's first kicks, knowing that child is being nurtured physically and emotionally from your body, giving birth—yes, it hurts but in a good way—and loving and caring for this new infant is a gift beyond description. And no less of a thrill when you hold your adopted child. It's your baby either way, because he or she is meant to be yours and will be forever.

The other good news is that many husbands and male partners are more supportive, nurturing and helpful than they used to be, partly due to the fact that more often now, both parents either choose or need to be in the work force. But enough of parenting! That's for the younger crowd. For an older woman, becoming a parent is likely a moot point. Sex isn't!

Some of my words and descriptions might sound blunt or at the very least, outdated. However, the groundwork must be laid … er, so to speak. Guys have always found it simpler and even more socially acceptable (blindness or mental decline aside) to pleasure themselves than the gals have. It's what they did and do. It's just easier for them. They have something to hang onto, and I don't think the fear of needing glasses, growing warts, or losing I.Q. concerns them anymore.

One gentleman shared that as a kid he used to "do it" in a sock so that his mother wouldn't know. Now with awareness and acceptance in full swing, little boys are apt to be told, "If you want to do that—and I know it feels good—just do it in your room in private." Fewer little girls were even aware there was anything but plumbing "down there" to be stimulated—certainly not in the same way as the guys. All this changes with puberty. But let's go back to the older woman.

Several years ago my friend Helen confided: *"It wasn't until I was 45 years old that I learned that women were not only able to experience this thing called orgasm, but that it was okay, desired and even to be expected — thank you, Ladies Home Journal! My husband was not a great lover, not even mediocre, and unfortunately, I had been unable to ask for more. You just didn't talk about it then,"* she said. *"Besides, I wouldn't have known what to ask for anyway. It wasn't a subject that a woman could feel comfortable discussing with another person, male or female."*

I've spoken with many older women whose sex lives left them feeling pretty much "used," aware that they were missing *something* from the activity that their mates certainly seemed to enjoy — they just didn't know what. It was just *the way it was* for so many women, and that's sad.

But, here's the good news: Since the 60's, more and more women have discovered the joys of sex and realize they're entitled to those joys. They are more willing to ask for what works for them, and whether single or married, they can darn well take care of their own sexual release all by themselves when necessary. Neither desire nor fulfillment have to end with an "I'm too old" if you don't want it to.

We can thank the Women's Liberation movement for allowing females to embrace the "use it or lose it" sentiment that had previously belonged to only the male of the species ... and, sometime in the 70's, they even cranked it up a notch with, "I'd rather have it wear out than rust out!" Ah, Women's Liberation ... so much more than bra burning!

Since we're not built like men — for which I'm truly grateful except when I'm caught short outdoors and have to maneuver a squat in the snow when skiing—we have to be more creative in our methods of self-stimulation and enjoyment. Let's be very clear here: I'm not a doctor or therapist. I don't even play one on TV, so the opinions and observations I share are strictly my beliefs and interpretations. Not science. Not gospel. Just more exploration of how to enjoy life to the fullest for just as long as humanly possible. A very logical thing to do, in my humble opinion.

I believe that intimacy is a very important piece of the discussion. Eighteen years ago, I was asked to write an article about it. Here's an excerpt:

Intimacy — one of the most important achievements in life is one of the most difficult to attain. You may think you have it in your relationship and then when a situation arises where you <u>really</u> experience it, you realize what's been missing and actually go through a mourning period for what you consider to be lost time ....

.... By the time I met Jim, I certainly knew the things I <u>didn't</u> want in a relationship, and at the top of the "must have and share" list was intimacy — emotional, physical, spiritual intimacy. I doubt I could have defined it then, but Jim was in pretty much the same place, so we found our intimacy together. But not without a few ups and downs!

My definition of achieving intimacy in a

relationship is that it's <u>not</u> painting a picture of what you'd like your life to be and then living the picture, nor is it playing roles to make others happy; both talents I excelled at. I've come to learn it's being honest and communicating with each other, not judging or feeling judged, knowing that you can be yourself in every way, and that you will be supported and loved in that place. It develops slowly as trust grows; trust in each other and in your emotions. It's acceptance that you are worthy of such gifts and allowing yourself to receive them. Intimacy means caring more for your partner's wellbeing than for your own but not giving your power away in the process.

Being vulnerable was a huge leap of faith for me, and I used to run back to what I called "my protective zippers." Luckily, trust grows when you respect and honor yourselves and each other for who and what you are. Intimacy is listening, and really hearing each other — emotionally, spiritually and physically. It's commitment, being able to experience emotions — anger, passion, sorrow and joy — and knowing beyond all doubt that your partner is there, and will continue to be there and love you; that your love will continue to grow through those experiences.

As Jim and I unzipped the layers of protection we had buried ourselves in, we were awed by the depth of feelings that we shared. And we still are, even after 30 years of marriage, because the intimacy *simply continues to expand. We've shared our feelings with our five children through the years and trust it's helped them in their relationships, too. At least the feedback has been inspiring! We've faced our challenges and no doubt will continue to — that's growth, and love, and why we're here.*

And now, back to our regularly scheduled program: SEX!

I believe that raw passion requires tempering with a bit of wisdom, and that sex is such a powerful thing, you can never go wrong with adding a *lot* of tenderness and affection. A genuine fondness for your partner is highly desirable, and worth developing as much as possible. And yes, for some people, pet names are allowable, and can even help.

But if the pet names don't work for you, and the physical act isn't happening with your partner, you can always take matters into your own hands … so to speak. I sometimes liken sex to a gas station … sometimes you get full service, sometimes you've got to ask for service, and sometimes you have to be happy servicing yourself.

Here I note that self-satisfaction in this chapter refers to the sexual variety, and if the idea makes you blush, just remember that our species has been indulging in such activities for a long, long time … the health benefits are legend!

Turns out that 4,000 years ago, Egyptian men were blaming the (what they perceived to be) mental disorders of Egyptian ladies on "wandering wombs." Yes, you read that right. Around 2,000 years ago, Hippocrates, the father of medicine, was still convinced that the womb could "wander" through the body, causing all sorts of trouble by blocking the flow of blood and fluids, and that this was the root cause of *hysteria* from the Greek *"υστέρα hystera"* which means uterus.

By the time The Renaissance rolled around, the "midwives" hired to "manually stimulate" hysterical women, were running up against the physicians, who, being higher up on the class ladder, were more influenced by the Church. The physicians' prescriptions were less *user-friendly*.

This might be the reason that in 1734, a mechanically gifted Frenchman invented the first mechanical, wind-up — yes, wind-up — with a key, no less — vibrator called the "Tremoussoir." Tonsil hockey *and* the first vibrator. You just gotta love the French!

Moving on to the Victorian Age. Even though Her Majesty, Queen Victoria, is usually associated with very puritanical practices, one must also note that she gave birth to nine children, and one source reports that she not only enjoyed looking at pictures of naked men, she sometimes indulged in drawing them! At any rate, British doctors were still merrily going about the treatment of "Female Hysteria" the old-fashioned way, by hand, until Dr. Joseph Mortimer Granville's invention of an electromechanical vibrator around 1880. If you haven't seen the movie "Hysteria," gather your girlfriends and pop some corn. It's a stitch.

Finally, we have to mention that the vibrator was the fifth "home appliance" to be electrified — after the sewing machine, the fan, the tea-kettle and the toaster, but about a decade before the vacuum cleaner and electric iron. I have a friend who named her vibrator Bob. I asked, "Who's Bob?" She smiled and said, "Boyfriend on batteries." Yes, times have changed.

We can probably agree that in most cases, a man, even a really selfless one, when involved in the act of making love, has two goals: #1. To bring his partner to a climax as soon as possible so that ... #2. He can get on with it and enjoy the same. And yes, there are lots of men who skip right over #1 with nary a thought. The books say that, usually, what takes a man two minutes takes a woman twenty.

This loving patience can be hard to come by (pun intended), and once he's discovered what works — what buttons to push to create the desired effect — he tends to stay with the routine. It's the "if it's not broke, don't fix it" thing. For the woman, this translates to being more about sex than lovemaking, and the same ol', same ol' then becomes boring and begins to feel more like … work. For both parties.

Looking in the mirror requires us to accept the fact that we women of a certain age have, indeed, changed. When our reflection has gained a little weight — seldom in the right places, and shows the effects of gravity — whoa! There go the boobs, headin' south! When hair grays and sometimes thins, and skin damage runs amok, we may want to hide under the covers. The good news is that by this *certain age,* we have also acquired wisdom, the ability to laugh at ourselves, and if we are open to it, and lucky, and truly, truly blessed, a relationship with trust as its foundation.

I remind you here that women aren't the only gender affected by the passing years. An image: He's brushing his teeth, what's left of them, as his potbelly hides one of his more interesting assets. The thrill of seeing his body naked … well, it just isn't what it used to be, now is it? He might be less apt to remember to chew with his mouth closed, or be a bit more … comfortable … about passing gas or burping. It doesn't help romance to flourish.

The good part is that true love sees past the outer shell. It doesn't go away, and the love of the soul within grows deeper with each passing year. What this couple is seeing in the mirror is simply the physical reflection of the aging of the shell, while the soul is screaming out, "That's not me! I don't feel that old and I don't want to lose that fulfilling joy of sex ... ever! Help!"

I've been told that Viagra and similar products have saved marriages, or at least one of the important aspects of them. Hurray! Unfortunately, not as much is being done for the female at this time. It's the double standard thing again, and the female mind needs to be acknowledged. It's a big sex organ. We can choose to just give him pleasure, or we can fake it ... and we all knew how to do that long before Sally ("When Harry Met Sally") showed how easy that is! The movie line was, "I'll have what she's having" but in reality, it's more like, "I'll have what *he's* having." One way or another, we women really do need the physical release just as much as men do.

Several women I've talked with have complained about premature ejaculation, a condition where the male orgasm happens way too fast. *Fifteen second penetration and it's over* can leave a girl totally frustrated and under the assumption that it's all her fault for not being able to "come" fast enough. Hello ... even in the male-centered world of *Wham, Bam, Thank You, Ma'am,* 15 seconds barely rates a "Wh...!"

Kathy, an older friend, had enrolled in a Human Sexuality class of 150 students many years ago. *"When the teacher referred to the 'Eleven*

Minute Man,' I raised my hand and asked what that
meant. I had no clue what they were talking about,
but was mightily embarrassed by the laughter of the
younger students!" With a sad smile, she admitted
to me that she still doesn't. Nor an eight or even a
six for that matter!

Nowadays, communication between lovers is
heartily encouraged, sex toys are readily available,
and literature, which was once banned or burned,
is available in hard, soft and digital formats. The
taboos about partaking in the pleasures of sex are
replaced with imaginative ways to get everyone
into the swing ... er ... act, and there are even
scholarly studies to prove the benefits.

Now back to single women not in a relationship,
and alternate methods of self-stimulation. Sexual
tension needs to be discharged; important parts
of the anatomy need exercise, and let's face it...
an orgasm feels awfully good! Making love with a
machine may not be ideal, but it's better than not
at all, right?

Dr. Ruth is an advocate of vibrators,
recommending one in particular, but sexual toys
today come in all shapes and sizes. Find one
that works for you and explore the possibilities.
Today's sex toys will wake you up in more ways
than one! From a tiny device to stimulate the
external clitoris, all the way to a full blown (so
to speak) appliance, your own personal vibrator

could be the secret to your success ... and just might erase some wrinkles from your brow.

And speaking of the clitoris, Sophia Wallace invented the term *cliteracy*. Clitoris Literacy. Did you know that the clitoris wasn't scientifically discovered until 1998?

Here's a word of advice: If you have a partner, include them in your discovery. Of course, he needs to be told it's not nearly as good as the real thing, and that he's infinitely better than "that thing." Explain that it's simply to take some pressure off his performance, maybe include it in your lovemaking, and assure him that it will allow him to just go for it when that's what's best for him...or you. Male egos can be vulnerable in this area, you know.

One gal—we'll call her "Happy"—told me she'd finally ordered a vibrator in the mail and was giving it a whirl.

"*It was fantastic,*" Happy whispered, "*until the time the battery ran out at just the wrong moment. Boy, was I ever cranky that day!*"

Then there's menopause, which can mess with your hormones, and that can mess with your sex drive. There are several herbs purported to enhance sexual drive; talk to your OB/GYN or other authority about them. One good friend says she uses damiana leaves ... and they "work!" Needless to say, losing the fear of pregnancy can make sex all the more free and exciting. Another avenue is to ask your doctor about some compounded testosterone cream. A tiny amount rubbed on the upper thighs, tummy or even directly on the clitoris has been known to increase a woman's flagging libido. The old Brylcreem ad line, "A little dab'll do ya" has a whole new meaning.

Anyone who remembers Bill Clinton will likely be able to guess the next topic, and here I will add that Barbara Bush was right: "A man might forget where he parks or where he lives, but he never forgets *oral sex,* no matter how bad it is." These days, almost anywhere you turn you'll hear or read about the BJ or "blow job." Years ago at a girls' night out, a newly divorced friend blushingly admitted that she had no idea how to accomplish that feat, but knew it was going to come up soon since she was dating a handsome young man. There was a fruit platter nearby with a lovely bunch of bananas, and I can assure you that with a little coaching from her friends, she soon had the knack of it!

Perhaps more intriguing to females is what is technically referred to as *cunnilingus.* Still oral sex, but on the woman. It's very important to get to know that part of your body, what it looks like and what feels good to *yours,* since you might need to do some gentle urging and directing someday. One woman told me that if she could, she would insure her husband's tongue. As she said it, she fanned her face with her hand and a blush crept up her cheeks.

Whichever way you may tip, relax and make sex another way of staying youthful and vibrant. As I said, if your sex life remains viable and fun, not only do *you* benefit, but the whole partnership improves. Try date nights or an afternoon of soft music, maybe a shower together, a glass of wine, a little lubricant and lots of communication. Songs of love are written just so you can hit the high notes.

Jim and I had a date planned, an "afternoon delight," when he returned from golf. The dog was out of the bedroom, soft music played, shades were drawn. We snuggled and cuddled, loved each other, and truly appreciated that we could still do it! Sighing with sweet memories, he jumped in the shower and I was looking for tossed clothes when I heard a male voice. "Judy! Judy, are you there?" Someone was at the front door!

I ran to the bedroom door and swung it open to see if I could tell who was there. Clad in bra and panties, I could see exactly who was there ... our gardener had stepped inside the entry room and, of course, was looking my way. (You need to know that when you walk in our front door, you have a direct view of not only our bedroom, but our bed. And now me.)

"Oh, I'm so sorry!"

"Oh, it's okay … I'll be right out," I squeaked. OMG, this is embarrassing!

He went back out the door, all 6'7" handsome guy that he is, and was patiently waiting for this somewhat disheveled, glowing, older woman to arrive.

"I hope I didn't wake you from a nap," he tactfully said, looking at his feet with just a hint of a twitch at the corner of his mouth.

I wanted to answer that that's not what we call it. But I didn't. It was all very cool and I'm sure we'll be able to look each other in the eye again someday!

You're never too old and it's never too late … honest. Any way you can accomplish it, good, sweaty, open, healthy sex can truly be an "afternoon delight!"

~EIGHT~

"You give little when you give of your possessions. It is when you give of yourself that you truly give."
Kahil Gibran (1883-1931)

A Friend—Indeed!

Someone once said that part of a best friend's job should be to immediately clear your computer history if you die. So true!

Friends come in all ages and sizes and none of that matters a whit. If you have a friend who's seen you through some of the good and bad times or just listens when you talk about them, you are indeed a lucky and blessed person. It could be a family member but sometimes it's not.

Female friendships are interesting relationships. They range from the acquaintance/friend level, all the way to those very special friends, precious for as long as you live, even when you don't see each other for months or years at a time. The bond between women begins with an inner core of understanding, and builds on sharing, strength, wisdom, endurance and love. A sisterhood. It's what gets us through those curves that life loves to throw at us.

Some relationships muddle along with Christmas-card-only notes, maybe with photos of kids, then grandkids. As we get older, it might be a note saying that someone has lost a loved one. An important sign of a deep forever friendship is to ask yourself who you would call in a big emergency; who would drop everything and come to your side, and for whom the reverse would be true. Those folks are few and far between. I've been told if you can count them on one hand, you're a very fortunate person.

Relationships with complete acceptance, in both directions, and no demands of change. It's being able to be completely honest with someone and not take offense if they're honest with you. That takes awhile to develop; acceptance instead of criticism or judgment. It also means supporting each other. You need to be able to ask for help and understanding, and they must be willing and able to do the same. "I didn't want to bother you" doesn't work.

I've experienced two marriages, one divorce, four childbirths, the loss of a son, and a major surgery. I thank God for the women and men who have supported me emotionally and physically through the laughter and tears. I hope I've done the same for them. I know that letting yourself get so wrapped up in the minutiae of daily life and losing touch with old friends can be a source of deep regret. There's guilt knowing that you didn't put in the time and effort old friends deserve, and staying in touch.

I know because I had a wonderful friend who lived 400 miles away. We were comfortable just seeing each other once a year with a few emails in between, and I hadn't talked to her in six months, too tied up in my own world. Then one day I kept feeling a deep need to call her and picked up the phone. Her husband answered and he was crying. It was too late. I had no idea she was even sick. It had come on quickly and she had been unable to even email. I do think she nudged, though. If you ever feel a tug to talk to someone, follow through on it. You just never know, and truthfully, life is not that full. I feel my friend and I are in touch on another level now, but it's not quite as satisfying as a real life hug.

As I'm writing, my mood has become quite pensive remembering old friendships. I'm going to suggest we, myself included, make a list of those people we've thought of getting in touch with, connecting with again, and haven't. Stop postponing and just do it! Stop procrastinating. Do it now before it's too late.

I was so grateful after my back surgery to have friends call or come by for a visit, sometimes bringing a meal. I suspect most of them knew that Jim isn't exactly known for his cooking, just for being an excellent caregiver. One dear friend and her husband brought a "prayer quilt" made by members of their church for me to take to the hospital. Each knot was lovingly tied while saying a prayer. It's beautiful. I cherish it, and it's surely one of the reasons I recovered so quickly.

Jim and I are close to several couples who love to play card games. We get together to play "Sequence" or "Mexican Train" while we share a meal or snacks, and always end up laughing 'til we cry. It's amazing how quickly we forget whatever bad stuff is going on in the world ... and that's such a relief. It's good to get away from the TV and off the computer for a while! Bridge is another great social gathering game, although I haven't played since college. We also meet up with friends at our local bistro once or twice a week to dance and sing and enjoy the wonderful musical group that plays there.

I sometimes feel like an analogue woman trapped in a digital world. Between computers and mobile phones and now iPads and tablets, well ... it's nearly impossible to function without them. They've changed our world, and as a writer, they definitely have had a huge effect on mine. Just the thought of having anything happen to my computer gives me an anxiety attack ... and everything's even backed up! I still don't know all the in's and out's of Windows 7 and along comes Windows 8. I shudder at the thought! Life was a lot simpler in the old days!

I swore I'd never read anything but paper pages … that was before I was gifted with a Nook. And of course my own books now exist in digital format. And I do play "Words with Friends" with my husband (after I made him promise not to look up spellings on the internet). So far so good … then along came smart phones.

I used to have a very small, easy to operate, comfortable cell phone which I kept in my pocket for emergencies only. Once in a great while my husband would call me on it if I didn't answer the home phone. I was okay with that. But, being digitally-minded, my mate just couldn't wait to upgrade his phone, and once that happened, he became very pushy about the inferiority of my communication gadgets. After weeks of what I call his slow-drip, water-torture technique, I succumbed and joined him at the store.

Jim: "*My wife needs a new phone. What do you recommend?*"

Salesperson: "*Well, hello. It's nice to meet you. I'm sure we have the perfect phones for you both.*"

Me: "*I doubt it. I like what I have,*" I said sulking.

Salesperson: "*Can you tell me what you use it for?*"

Me: "*I don't. I carry it when I go walking in case I have an emergency.*"

Salesperson: "*Oh. Well, what do you think you'll do with a new one?*"

Jim: "*She needs a keyboard.*"

Salesperson: "*Oh, no problem. They all have that. And the touch is so easy.*"

Me: "*No it's not. My fingers are too big, my thumbs don't move like that. If I type a message on that, it looks like a foreign language and needs translating. I need to have the feel of actually punching a key.*"

Salesperson: "*Oh, don't you worry. We'll find something for you.*" (*Mumbled under his breath*) "*She's going to be a challenge.*"

Me: (*under my breath*) "*I could be ...*" and gave Jim one of 'those looks.'

After looking at a dozen choices and hearing a few heavy-duty pitches made by the two men, I ended up with a huge, heavy, awkward phone with a pull-out key board.

Salesperson: "*Now, what apps would you want?*"

I noted that his cheeks were getting red.

Me: "*What's an app?*"

Salesperson looked at Jim with pleading eyes that said, "Help!"

At long last, we got everything all put together and I slipped the new phone into my pocket … and darn near fell over! It barely fit, and I looked totally deformed.

Me: *"Good grief! I can't carry this thing around all the time!"*

Salesperson: *"We have some very attractive cases which allow you to wear it on your belt."*

Me: *"I haven't worn a belt in years. I've shrunk so much, I don't have a waist anymore!"*

Salesperson: *"Oh. Well. You could put it in your handbag or a fanny pack."*

Me: *"I'd never hear it in my pocketbook and I don't really need to pack anything more on my fanny."* By now, it was a toss-up as to whether I or the sales guy was more frustrated.

About then, Jim stepped up to the plate. *"Come on, kiddo."* (His one and only term of endearment.) *"I'll show you how to use it."*

By the end of two weeks, I was ready to throw the damn thing in the lake.

Me: *"I hate it. I don't want it. I can't even use this keyboard. It was a bad choice."*

Jim: *"OK, call the store and return it."* (My honey was practicing patience).

Back at the phone store …

Salesperson: *"Oh yes, I remember you. Now when did you buy this phone?"*

I told him.

Salesperson: "*Gee, that's too bad. If it was within two weeks, we could exchange it. But it's now been 15 days. That's too late.*"

I can't print what went through my mind. Well, I guess, considering some of what's been in print and the media of late, I could, but I'll spare you. Besides, you likely get the drift … smoke was coming out of my ears, nose, eyes and mouth, and let me just say that it's a darn good thing I'm a peace-loving person.

It's been six months, and I've learned a few things about my new phone. I can now answer it, for one thing. I've managed to take a few photos which sadly weren't printable after I finally located them. That only took two days. I much prefer my small camera anyway.

Could the issues be about me and my personality? I am a Taurus after all. Possibly to do with my heritage and being a bit stubborn by nature? The difficulties of teaching an old dog new tricks? Yeah, that too. Ask Jim. He'll confirm it. What can I say? I'm learning … or at least trying to.

While we're talking about all this, I will also say that I really don't like the changes in communication that are taking place for other reasons than just the hardware. I do not like that these changes are building a wall of isolation, removing all human senses from what passes as communication, even talking on the telephone.

It's all about texting and that's a problem. Kids do it in school, it's done in cars while driving—a very dangerous, stupid thing to do. I guess I'm just old-fashioned.

Albert Einstein knew what I'm talking about when he said, *"I fear the day when the technology overlaps with our humanity. The world will only have a generation of idiots."* Photos of such idiocy abound … four women having lunch *together*, all texting instead of talking, a *date* with the boy and girl sitting on a couch texting each other. Doubtless the wedding by text isn't far off, if it hasn't happened already! Same texting scenario with kids at a beach, obviously having a desire to see each other, but they're not *seeing* each other. And let me tell you folks, when the young men give up ogling the young ladies in bikinis in favor of playing with their electronics, the world is in serious trouble!

Will this soon be what passes for the connections we used to have with friends? If I hadn't seen the scenes for myself, I wouldn't have believed it, but we need to address our disconnection; the loss of not looking a friend in the eye and reading how they really feel about something through those windows to the soul.

All that said, in the interest of full disclosure, I will admit I'd be lost without email, and that I'm a little addicted to Facebook … but I have no idea how to access them on my cell phone, nor do I want to! Sigh. I guess that's my rant for the day!

It is said that the true value of friendship cannot be measured, but treasured. If you are among those fortunate few who can lay claim to good or best friends, you know that this is absolutely correct. You can have many kinds of friends from childhood, school, work; acquaintances and friends of friends. You may strike up an instant relationship with somebody, but it may take years for you to really know that person.

When you can speak your mind freely without donning an artificial smile, without worrying about calling anytime, and without worrying about being judged, you will know that you have a friend for life. Indeed, good friends make life worth living.

So back to girlfriends … the first quality to look for is the ability to accept you as you are, without seeking to change you in any way. No pretending allowed. If your friend comments on what you do or say and judges you at the drop of a hat with no regard for your motivations or feelings, she is likely not good friend material. The cornerstone of good friendship is complete acceptance. Your happiness makes her happy too. If you have a friend who finds joy in your success and never gets jealous, you indeed have a good friend.

True friends can gauge when you are happy, sad, excited, shocked or upset. If you are down in the dumps, your friend will know how to make you happy and put a smile on your face. And if she can't, as one of those silly emails that cycles around every year or two says, she'll sit and trash the bums who made you feel bad in the first place.

So bottom line, cell phones are great for many reasons, but don't forget the value of face-to-face sharing, whether it's good news or bad news ... or just to hear their voice. Go meet for a latté now, and then take a walk together, appreciate what goes on in her life and honor what goes on in yours.

Personally, I intend to live a long healthy life ... gotta keep those good friends!

~NINE~

"You never know what you have till you've lost it."
Alyson Noel, Evermore

Loss—A Fact of Life

But that doesn't make it any easier. The older
we get, the more loss we've experienced.
I, like all my friends at this age, have suffered
painful losses — partners, parents, children, family,
friends, and let's not forget the pets, jobs, homes,
and even those really, really comfortable earrings
you splurged on to celebrate whatever it was
you'd done, and now one of them has gone
missing. Death, illness, and divorce are the really
big causes. And since this is definitely not a light-
hearted chapter, I will keep it short. Suffice to say
that for me, survival comes down to beliefs, the
spiritual beliefs that keep me going.

After I wrote my first book, a metaphysical/
spiritual adventure novel called *EarthShift*, an
amazing number of readers contacted me and shared
their own metaphysical/spiritual experiences.
That was both revealing and enlightening. Those

readers' stories and my own may, one day, be another book, but for now, I'll just say that it's my belief that the spirits of loved ones remain around us for a long time after their deaths, becoming — yes, guardian angels is a reasonably accurate term — and watching over us, our children, whoever was and is important to them.

We've all heard stories of people seeing ghosts, hearing voices, or just having *a knowing,* and a great number of us find comfort in these things. There are many wonderful books that can bring some degree of peace and acceptance to those left behind. Some people have talismans, keep special photos close at hand, or keep special rituals, and of course, for all of us, there are memories that can't be taken away.

More and more gifted people are now acknowledged for their exceptional abilities to "see," "hear," or "know" what departed beings wish to share with their loved ones. This can be an amazing and helpful gift, but you need to be very aware that there are many charlatans out there. Discernment — the simple judgment of such a gifted person, and the degree of that person's gift to "discern the spirits" — is incredibly important. A lot of money is wasted and hopes dashed searching in the wrong places for those connections.

I've communicated with the son I lost to spina bifida in various ways through the years, but that's a private experience and mine alone. The world is becoming more open to these spiritual possibilities, although in other countries more than ours. As far as I'm concerned, it's *to each his own*. There are many stories I could share, but not in this book. I do feel that time—lots of time—heals much pain, although that's hard to accept when the pain is fresh and raw. Time for grieving is a necessary step in recovery, the time when close family and friends are vital to our survival, and there is no universal timetable.

One thing that strikes me as odd, and seems to stand out in general conversations is that there's less fear of death than we might think. But there is a fear of how death will come, and great concern about the personal and family suffering involved, whether death comes slowly or quickly. My wish is to have as few regrets as possible.

To that end, I would offer the following list of Regrets To Avoid:

1. For both men and women, don't work so hard that you miss the joy of your kids' youth or the companionship of your partner. Admittedly, we have to make a living to be able to take care of the family, but your presence is more important than all the toys and trips and trifles. Money will probably be the last thing you'll wish for in your last days of life. It's the memories and the time.

2. I already touched on friends and the

importance of staying in touch. Remember that you can't go back.

3. Be true to yourself. I spent so many years trying to be the person my parents thought I should be. There must have been a rebellious kid in there somewhere! And later, trying to be (apologies to Julianna Margulies) the good wife. I might have accomplished that early on, but to the detriment of my dreams. I think I was a pretty good mom, at least that's what I'm told! Learn to speak up and ask for what you feel you deserve. I'm better at this now.

4. Laugh! We need to laugh more. It's a complicated issue because there are no secret buttons to push, no jokes to read, movies to watch, to magically make it happen. Honest laughter comes from deep within and massages everything from sole to soul. It's really, truly good for you. I can tell you from experience that when you've been spending a lot of time alone and a hearty laugh escapes, it can come as a big surprise.

Not for everyone. I'm a quiet laugher. Some laugh constantly but it's not necessarily from the heart. And some are gifted to be just plain happy folks, seeing the cup half full all the time. That's not saying they don't have pain and suffering in their lives ... that's called living ... but they're just plain happy folks.

~TEN~

"The secret of staying young is to live honestly, eat slowly, and lie about your age."

Lucille Ball

Love, Life and Laughter

L ove and laughter are indispensable parts of a good, healthy life. I'm fortunate to have plenty of both in mine, from Jim, our children, family and friends, not to mention our pets. You can't beat pets for unconditional loving, entirely without expectations ... well, besides the kibble and the occasional biscuit of course! As is said, you only hope you're half as wonderful as your dog thinks you are!

I think, especially given our constant bombardment with "late-breaking news," we could all use more laughter in our lives. For many reasons, the good old belly laughs don't come around as often as they used to when we were uninhibited youngsters.

I remember gathering my boys together, all lying on the floor, everyone with their head on

114

another one's belly. It's such a silly scene, but as soon as someone starts laughing, thanks to bouncing tummies, all are soon convulsed in laughter. You just can't help it. What a catharsis!

It takes an extremely funny email to make me laugh or even giggle out loud these days. However, when I do, I share the message and hope someone else will feel the same way. It happens so seldom, I sometimes wonder if I've lost my sense of humor!

When we get together with friends, we tend to let it loose more often and laugh to the point of tears, frequently at my expense, since I tend to say dumb things or come up with unintentional innuendos now and then ... and I laugh the hardest of all.

Freedom of behavior matches up with younger ages, but hear me now ... we're never too old!

Years ago, while vacationing at the seashore in Maine, we were spending an evening at my brother's cottage with his wife and kids, ages four and six, and our parents. It was pouring. The adults were enjoying vodka gimlets and listening to the rain on the roof. My sister-in-law and I went into the kitchen to make some dinner, and the kids, with their big beautiful blue eyes, had followed us in, pleading to go out in the rain. Our first reaction was, "No ... you'll get wet." Well, of course they would!

One of us—I like to think it was me—then said, "Well, why not? We won't melt!" We snuck out with the kids, grabbed their hands and acted silly in the yard. We remembered it was high tide, so with a feeling of great conspiracy, went skipping down the muddy road, jumping in puddles on our way to the beach, where we splashed into the cold salty water with our clothes and shoes on, and played "ring-around-a-rosy" in the dark until we were exhausted from laughing at ourselves. Drenched and happy, we sloshed back up the road. The expressions on my brother's and parent's faces were ones of incredulous disbelief as we stood, making enormous puddles in the little kitchen. But the kids' faces lit up the whole room. The memory is priceless. We had laughed and splashed and played ... and for that time, the world had stood still.

Personally, I want to feel that feeling! Again and again! And I have! With my own grandkids. In all manner of weather.

I think that rain and snow must loosen particularly joyous emotions which allow something ... almost forbidden, to be felt. Case in point: Two of the grandkids were visiting us and wanted to go out in the rain and sleet. "Well, why not? In fact, let's all go! I'll get the camera!"

Another time, two little ones from Vegas were here with us, watching the snow fall. It was about bedtime, but there was such longing etched on their faces. I looked at their parents, crossed my fingers, and asked the kids if they'd like to go out with me and make snowmen. Their reactions didn't allow for any dissention! Their daddy got into it and soon, snowballs were flying, as mom took photos of snow-encrusted kids and the hilarious snowmen we'd made. Have you ever caught big snowflakes on your tongue? Delicious! It was such a great night.

It all comes down to love, laughter and life. The older we get, the more restrictions we put on ourselves. It just happens. When I hear that nasty refrain, "I'm too old" in my head, I have to physically stop, scold myself, and pivot. I remind myself that I'm never too old! I admit that sometimes you wonder if the body will hold up; that's valid. Just because lots of body parts can be repaired or replaced, doesn't mean it's the thing to do! It's much better to not have to!

About 14 years ago (eons!), my son and daughter-in-law asked if I could baby-sit for a week. She was going out of the country and he would be on a big business trip. Of course I could! I had to fly there—always a bit stressful for me—but I got big hugs from the three young-uns when I landed, which made it all worthwhile. The kids were about 5, 7 and 9. I'll call them A, B, and C. Girl, boy and boy, and just full of it. I wrote the following email to family and friends when I got home ...

Just a note to let you know I'm home and that not only did I survive the week, I really enjoyed myself. BUT ... I am exhausted!! I've played more games than I knew existed, read more books, recalled what transporting kids to different places at the same time was really like, re-learned the art and necessity of distraction, lost my temper just once (thank you "B"), didn't panic at screams or wails, got lots of hugs, and decided that whatever it was that they ate for one week wouldn't kill them. Rome was not built in a day.

I've watched zillions of cartoons and videos but had no idea if the world outside of the house was at war or burned up. And I learned how incredibly smart my grandchildren are ... and what awesome memories they have, especially when it's something you would prefer they forget.

I've been in another time zone, and it was not Eastern, Central, Mountain or Pacific! I was always so sure there was never enough time to get all the things done I needed to do ... well, this week I experienced time standing still or going so slowly that I truly thought something was wrong with my watch ... But it was 2:15 an hour ago ... how can it only be 2:20? or Good Lord! You kids should have been in bed two hours ago! Your parents will kill me!

So I'll pick up the mail from the PO this morning, try to get the smell of the long-dead mouse out of the kitchen cabinet, buy some fruit and veggies and delete hundreds of emails. Then I'll take a deep breath and listen to the silence .... ah, heaven!

Love, Mom/Judy

PS: I was gifted with a golf-shirt with a beautifully embroidered angel on it and "Grammy" underneath it. That, along with the piece of highly prized (although somewhat finger-printed) piece of gum from "B" at the airport, made it all worthwhile!

I still have and proudly wear that shirt. The gum was lost during our last move, and those kids are pretty much grown up now. But the memories of that week, whether stressful or joyful, are forever in my heart.

Everyone needs something to look forward to, a reason to get up every morning. We need to keep learning, keep moving, keep walking, and being outside to soak up our requirement of vitamin D from the sun. Expect that something really good is going to happen in a day and it probably will. Attitude makes a world of difference, and a difference in the world.

Give up any regrets you might have about not having done certain things and just go do them, if you can! If you can't, pick something else. You never know when it might be too late to enjoy something you love due to any number of circumstances — physical, geographic, or financial.

For instance, there's absolutely nothing wrong with going out to eat by yourself, or going to the movies, or a play, or the museum, or whatever, whether you're a single gal or married. I know this because my husband travels a great deal, and I make sure to have some plans for my alone time … at home or elsewhere.

Pick a project. When we downsized six years ago, we had to get rid of so much "stuff." I made many trips to the resale store, charity places, and the dump. But we de-cluttered. We were staying in the same town, in fact, just five miles away, but with all the packing and flights of stairs in both houses, I lost 7 pounds! (Regretfully I found them again.) Now, this house needs to be sorted out and redistributed, and I have so many excuses to avoid doing it … even when I know that it always feels good to lighten the load.

When I feel overwhelmed with too much to do, pulled in too many directions, too many deadlines to meet, I pick just one thing to accomplish that day. Deciding on that one thing can break the log jam and get you moving … little steps. A friend in Maine makes herself a cup of tea and works on a given project "until the tea is gone." It's a strategy which breaks even a huge job into doable pieces, and getting things done reinforces the positive in life.

A smile turns a frown into a happy face, but one huge obstacle to feeling like smiling is worry. Worry shows in the face, it raises the blood pressure, and generally puts a damper on everything else in your life. There is a big worrier in our household, and it's me.

I tend to worry way too much about big things, little things, just every damn thing, and often have to remind myself, "Is it something I can do anything about?" And you know … nine times out of ten, it's not. Remembering to ask the question helps, but not all the time. I'm a work in progress. How about you? Are you a worrywart? Think of ways to let this go. And don't forget to smile!

Finding things to be thankful for and looking on the bright side really helps reinforce a positive outlook. Many songs were written on these themes back in the day. "Count Your Blessings" was one, "Accentuate The Positive," "Always Look On The Bright Side of Life." I'll stop short of "Cockeyed Optimist," but I know it's there!

Seriously, though, take a minute at the end

of the day and try to recall a few things that make you grateful, because gratitude is a powerful and very positive emotion.

Many years ago — almost 20 — one of our sons and his fiancée were planning their wedding. They asked to have it at our house, a pretty setting up in the hills above Los Angeles.

We all worked so hard to put things together. Jim and I got some landscaping done, made room for the caterers to spread out in the garage, welcomed friends and relatives, and before we knew it, the big weekend arrived. Beautiful tables were set up out back to accommodate 100 guests, a dance floor had been laid down, balloons had been blown up and hung. All was in readiness. Whew.

We gals were in the bedroom getting the excited and nervous bride into her gown, totally unaware of the drama taking place elsewhere. You see, we lived in the country and our water was supplied by our own well and a couple of huge holding tanks on the property.

Jim was dressed in his dark suit, trying to get the males organized, when his daughter grabbed his arm and whispered that she had gone to take a shower and there wasn't any water!

We panicked! Caterers coming, 100 guests, and … no water? OMG! We couldn't tell anyone, but there I was, madly trying to think of neighbors who might open their doors … and bathrooms! Hyperventilating more than a little, I was trying to be joyful with the bride-to-be while Jim ran down to the well house which was full of cobwebs — black widows yet! — old furniture and other crap. He crawled through it, but found no sign of anything wrong.

He then raced up to check the equipment housed at the top of the hill by the big storage tanks. He opened a little gizmo called the solenoid … and there, pinioned between the contacts, was an earwig. It had gotten stuck (and fried) between the connectors. Jim popped out the carcass and … we had water!

Of course by then, Jim needed a shower; sweating profusely … it was hot … and covered with cobwebs. The hero of the hour! Lots of brushing, deep breathing, thanking God for small favors followed. Very few of either family or guests knew about our close call that day, but it's a fond memory for me … one you just could not make up!

Another love, laughter and life memory …

For the same event, we had put our two dogs inside the paddleball court to keep them, and us, out of trouble. We didn't take into consideration that an adorable 4-year-old young man, all dolled up in a tux, would make it his mission to set them free. No one noticed when he opened the gate … or if they did, they said nothing.

But not long after, all I saw was our Golden Retriever, leaning as far over the new retaining wall as she could possibly stretch, with her nose about two inches from the top of the wedding cake. We caught her just in time but I must have lost ten years growth right then and there!

Memories, good and bad, are what life is about. Laughter plays such a huge part. We can all come up with hundreds of joyous events, disasters — some averted, some not, happy endings, and yes, some not so happy endings, lessons learned, steps taken.

So think about what you've learned, and what you can do to break the old patterns that aren't working for you. Life, as we know it, is short. Maybe we come back to do it again, maybe not.

Time spent now making changes to increase your happiness, to honor yourself, to make the choices you may have to make, and find enjoyment of your life in all ways possible is important time… time you owe yourself.

As I've said before, I truly believe you're only as old as you feel, and it's never too late. You may have days when you feel a heck of a lot older, but work on changing your thoughts and beliefs—making that 180° pivot—and you can change your life ... and that's where joy lives.

Be compassionate, be loving, and be happy!

Also by Judith Horky

*EarthShift – The Ancients Called it
The Shift of the Ages*

Soul Shift – 2012 and Beyond

By now, you pretty much know all there is to know about Judith Horky and her husband Jim! They feel totally blessed to have each other and to be enjoying life, dancing, friends, and their dog, Jesse. The mountains and lakes of Colorado bring them joy and peace as well as golf (for Jim), and writing (for Judy). Their family of 5 kids and 8 grandchildren along with other assorted relatives are scattered across the country, so they cherish their visits, whether at home or in cities from Maine to San Francisco. And they both agree whole-heartedly with the title of this book. Just remember ...

"You're never too old and it's never too late to be Ageless!"